I0150327

The Godly Household Manager

Wisdom and Encouragement for Wives and Mothers

By Kahteela D. Euseary

Fire Pens
Publishing

Detroit, Michigan

All passages are from the King James Version (KJV) of the bible.

Back Cover Author Photograph: Timashion Jones of TBOP Media

ISBN 978-0-692-95406-5

Copyright © 2017

All rights reserved. No part of this publication may be reproduced, distributed, or transmitted in any form or by any means, including photocopying, recording, or other electronic or mechanical methods, without the prior written permission of the publisher, except in the case of brief quotations embodied in critical reviews and certain other noncommercial uses permitted by copyright law. For permission requests, email the publisher, subject "Attention: Permissions Coordinator," at the email address below.

Printed in the United States of America

Acknowledgements

The Lord has chosen me as a vessel to distribute His wisdom but it does not always come as divine impartation. He has given me an ear to hear the wisdom of those who have more experience than I do. My parents taught me to listen to those who have traveled the path before me. I was taught to remain humble and to never cease learning.

I go through life gleaning from those who bear righteous fruit. I have learned a lot from other women. Some have given me verbal instructions and some have taught me through their actions. I am grateful to all who took the time to share with me their knowledge, wisdom, experience, and testimonies. I collect the raw materials then the Holy Spirit refines them through me.

I am blessed to have many family members who support me, Kardell and the children. They fight for us with all their might. The Lord saw fit to add to our support system even more people who love us and want to see us thrive. We could never have made it on our own. Thank God for His people.

The Holy Spirit gives me great wisdom. With this wisdom, I understand that I am *not* wise.

Prologue

Initially, my vision for this book was for it to be a fun and simple guide to household management for wives and mothers. I wanted to share tips on how to balance the many demands of the home. As I began to write, the Holy Spirit gave me a much deeper understanding of those things which I thought I understood. I realized that the book was not so much about managing a house in the natural, but more so about how our spiritual condition is manifested in the home. Much of the content in this book I learned as I wrote it. I prayed that The Lord would make me credible to the recipients of this message, and *that* He did through fiery trials. He was in the furnace with me and He brought me out without even the smell of smoke on my clothes. I came out with more wisdom and greater authority. If this book is an encouragement or answer to anyone's prayer, and if God be glorified, then I will tally every tear, every difficult season, and every moment of darkness, and count it all joy.

Contents

Introduction

Being a wife and mother has been, inarguably, the most demanding job in the world, both now and in times past. It is a job that requires constant mental, emotional, spiritual, and physical work. There never seems to be enough time in a day and the tasks never end. Those who receive the fruit of your labor may not always express gratitude and may never fully understand what you go through to make it all happen. It seems nearly impossible to maintain so many areas of the family's life and still keep ourselves both spiritually and physically well. The truth is that God has equipped us with all that we need to manage a godly household. In order to bring out the best in us, we must subject our thoughts and actions to the word of God. We must also listen and take heed to the wisdom of experienced godly women.

There is no doubt that the roles of mother and wife are difficult, but they bare additional weights that are not necessary to carry. The struggle is more than endless dishes and a washer that never stops. Much of the struggle is in the mind and in the heart.

In the second chapter of the book of Genesis, God created man. God made Adam from the dust of the earth and breathed his breath into his nostrils. Adam had intimate fellowship with Him. The Lord walked with him, talked with him, and taught him about his environment. God said that it was not good that Adam be alone, so He created Eve of Adams own body to be a help meet. Take note that they were not created at the same time. When God brought Eve to Adam, it marked the beginning of the institution of marriage. The Lord gave them permission to eat whatever they wanted from the garden, except from the tree of knowledge of good and evil. In chapter 3, we see the fall of mankind. Adam and Eve disobeyed God's commandment concerning the forbidden tree. Eve decided to go over to the tree that she was to stay away from, and she had a conversation with Satan who was speaking through a serpent. This passage is critical:

[1] Now the serpent was more subtle than any beast of the field which the Lord God had made. And he said unto the woman, Yea, hath God said, Ye shall not eat of every tree of the garden?
[2] And the woman said unto the serpent, we may eat of the fruit of the trees of the garden:
[3] But of the fruit of the tree which is in the midst of the garden, God hath said, Ye shall not eat of it, neither shall ye touch it, lest ye die.
[4] And the serpent said unto the woman, Ye shall not surely die:
[5] For God doth know that in the day ye eat thereof, then your eyes shall be opened, and ye shall be as gods, knowing good and evil.
[6] And when the woman saw that the tree was good for food, and that it was pleasant to the eyes, and a tree to be desired to make one wise, she took of the fruit thereof, and did eat, and gave also unto her husband with her; and he did eat.
[7] And the eyes of them both were opened, and they knew that they were naked; and they sewed fig leaves together, and made themselves aprons

Notice how the serpent starts the dialogue. He begins by asking a question. "Yea, God said that ye shall not eat of every tree of the garden"? This question was a luring question. It suggests suspicion on the part of the subject and sparks the curiosity of the listener. Let me make this idea more clear.

You are familiar with the TV scenarios where a detective questions two people separately, and they each are trying to protect each other. Imagine a man comes home late one evening. His wife accepts his explanation that he was in the office. Now, what if the detective says to her, "Did he tell you that he was at work last night?" Immediately, the wife would let down her guard. She will want to hear more because it sounds like there is a possibility that she has been lied to. From that point forward, the investigator will have control of her mind and he will be able to easily manipulate her and get her to believe anything that he says. This is what the serpent was doing.

Eve already knew that she was not to touch or eat from the tree. She confidently tells the serpent what God had said. In verse 4, the enemy responds *"Ye shall not surely die."* He directly opposed God's word! This was the first time that Eve had heard differently than what God said. I imagine that she was surprised and confused. Yet, she was interested to hear more. The serpent goes on to convince, "For God doth know that in the day that ye eat thereof, then your eyes shall be opened, and ye shall be as gods knowing good and evil." In this statement the enemy delivers two powerful blows that sealed the deal:

    A. He *convinces* Eve that God is withholding something good from them.

    B. He *persuades* Eve to pursue a "better" life.

    Eve then takes another look at the tree. She sees that it looks good and she desired to be wise so she decided to eat the fruit. She then took it to Adam and he eats it as well. As a result, sin entered the world and the whole creation fell.

God loved Adam and Eve. He gave them an amazing place to live, and most importantly, He gave them life. So, when the serpent directly opposed God's word, she should have run. Instead, she perked her ears and listened for more. After the serpent tells her that she would become

wise, she came to a turning point that cannot be overlooked. Eve changed her worldview. This was the goal of the tactic. Pay close attention to the fact that the serpent never told her to eat the fruit. He simply planted a seed of doubt in her mind because he knew that once she put God's word aside, she would inevitably choose evil. She went from seeing the tree as no good, forbidden, and deadly to seeing it as good for food and desirable. Eve ceased to see the world through the lens of God's word and began to see the world through the new lens offered by the enemy. With this change in view, it was easy for her to disobey God. In her mind, it was not disobedience. When she changed the way she saw things, she did what she thought was right. Eve was deceived.

Eve was Adam's wife, companion, help meet; literally, the only woman in the world for him. She took this fruit to her husband. Adam knew exactly what he was doing but he succumbed to the voice of his wife. The result was devastation. The enemy targeted Eve because he knew that she was the weaker vessel and more prone to deception. However, she had the ear of her husband. He knew that if he could get Eve to eat, she would get Adam to eat, and he would successfully gain authority in the earth. His goal was to destroy what God had done. Thousands of years later, the plan is the same, but the methods have gotten craftier.

The enemy has never ceased to try to deceive women with the exact methods that he used in Eden all those years ago. Just like he did Eve, he gets us while we are alone, when we are away from our husbands or people who will encourage us in the word. He opposes God's word and tells us that God is holding something back from us. We begin to feel like we are being hindered, like our dreams are dying, like our talents are being wasted, like our identities are lost. The enemy tells us that we could be happier, more successful, and more liberated if only:

  …you could follow your dreams.

  …you had your own money.

  …you did not have these children.

  …you did not have to submit to your husband.

Women of God, the enemy has been trying to lure us away from our families and our homes with bait. Bait in the form of a job, an education, an extramarital relationship, hopes and dreams, freedom from children, and indulgences. He begins by casting seeds of doubt; doubt that God has a plan for us and that He will allow us to express every gift and talent that we possess; doubt that He cares about our hopes and dreams. Once we put the Word aside, his work is complete because we will work to our own demise by leaning on our own understanding. We are sinful beings. So, when the word is not working in our lives, by default, we will make foolish and selfish decisions. There is nothing that Satan can offer us that does not already belong to us and will be manifested in God's timing. He has been stealing from us and selling us our own stuff. Sad to say, he has had much success through no greater tactic than the Women's Liberation Movement.

One of the foremost issues that come to mind is that of women's rights in the workplace. In 1941, during World War II over fifteen million men left home to become soldiers. About 350,000 women served on and off U.S soil. As a result, droves of women entered the workforce to fill in for men and to earn a living for their families. They took over jobs that normally only a man would do; factory jobs, especially. They took on jobs that not only put food on the table, but kept America running, and provided supplies and services to the military. Unfortunately, their employers refused to pay them what they paid men. When the men returned home, things did not go back to the way they were. Many women were abruptly laid off so that men could have their jobs back. Some remained in the

workforce because they had gotten a taste of a life that they wanted to keep.

This created a powerful social movement that would only pick up momentum over the years. Women were angry. They felt used and unappreciated. After they courageously stepped up to keep things going on the home front, they were pushed aside. This, no doubt created tension in families as well.

Imagine a homemaker wife finds out that her husband will be going to war for an unknown period of time. It may be years. He may never return. So, she steps up to the plate and gets a job. She finds someone to take care of her children. She will no longer be able to keep her house as clean or have much time to cook. It's scary, but she does it.

The job pays less than it paid men, but it's just temporary. It's enough to get by. As she adjusts to her new role in the household, she begins to like it. The role of provider is a lot of pressure, but for the first time, she is able to control money and make decisions. Maybe she realizes that because she is wise with money, she is able to do more than her husband did with less income. If she wants to buy a pair of shoes, she can do it without having to ask her husband first. The feeling of making a purchase with money from her own sweat gives her great satisfaction. It's not easy, but eventually she learns how to balance work, children, cooking, and cleaning. Then things change.

The war is over and the men come back. The employer says, "Sorry, we no longer need you." Her husband says, "thanks babe, for holding it down." As she returns back to her normal role in the household, she realized that she has changed and feels differently about being a homemaker.

Now, she has full knowledge of what it meant to be a provider, as well as a household manager. She is more critical of her husband's decisions. She expects him to do more around the house. After all, she did it all while he was gone, so there's no excuse. She has gained a set of skills that gives her the freedom to go out and get a job again. She no longer feels dependent on him.

This model represents the shift in thinking that propelled the Women's Liberation Movement. Many women remained in the workforce and dealt with inequality in wages as well as policies. The frustration only grew over the next two decades. When the Women's Liberation Movement was created in 1960, it marked the culmination of all that women had been fighting for.

Surely women ought to be treated equally to men. It is not fair to pay a woman less money for the exact same job just because she is a woman. Nor is it fair to deny women rights and privileges as a citizen that men have. So then, what is the problem? What is wrong with 'Lady Lib'? The problem is that the movement addressed the legitimate concerns for women's rights, but the overall agenda came from the mind of the enemy.

Women were truly being treated as second class citizens. The pain and frustration that they experienced was being used to propel the movement. As with any social movement, if you only focus on your own interests, and not question the final goal, you may very well be advancing an agenda that will ultimately harm you.

The world may be okay with a woman putting her family aside to pursue her own desires. The Lord is not. He is searching for a remnant of women who are willing to turn their hearts back to the home and put their families first. He wants His daughters to gain all of the knowledge and skills necessary to be who He has called them to be: the support of her husband, the nurturer to her children, the servant of the house, the spiritual watchman and tone setter of the home, The Godly Household Manager.

Chapter 1

Where Is a Woman's Place?

You have heard people say "A woman's place is in the home." You have also heard "you can have it all." Which one is true? Let us figure out exactly where a woman's place is in the home.

In the 1950s and before, it was the norm for women to stay home. Their number one priority was to take care of their husbands and children, and maybe do some church work, too.

Fast-forward to the 1980s and beyond, it was the norm for women to go back to school, start careers, and work full time jobs, then come home and take care of their families.

As the years go by, the so-called Women's Liberation movement has made tremendous progress. From a biblical standpoint, this progress has been destructive to the family. It went from gender equality to gender confusion, and from men are not superior to "we don't need men at all." The purpose of the Women's Liberation Movement was to destroy the family. The positive achievements cannot negate this fact. The fight has become not only about fairness, but about proving that women can do it all without a man. Women possess skills that are greatly needed in the home. The world is in desperate need of mothers returning home to be what God called them to be.

Proverbs 31 talks about the virtuous woman. This is a wife and mother that sets the bar high. This passage is referenced to outline the ideal woman. It is not a mandate, but an example of what to aim for:

To wives, mothers and those aspiring to be: know that your heart must be in the home. Your first ministry is your family. You are to serve and obey your husbands. You are to nurture and teach your children.

[16]She considereth a field, and buyeth it: with the fruit of her hands she planteth a vineyard. [17] She girdeth her loins with strength, and strengtheneth her arms.[18]She perceiveth that her merchandise is good: her candle goeth not out by night.[19] She layeth her hands to the spindle, and her hands hold the distaff.

The virtuous woman is a working woman. She works very hard and she brings money into her household. So, with this passage of scripture we can safely say that women earning money is a good thing. So, how do you figure out whether or not you should work outside the home or when to go back to work? Or perhaps, go to school?

To wives, mothers, and those aspiring to be: know that your heart must be in the home. Your first ministry is your family. You are to serve and obey your husbands. You are to nurture and teach your children. This is your primary responsibility. You may work outside of the home, but this does not relieve you of your primary duty. You may stay at home, but that is not the same as building a home.

To work or not to work? That is the question. How do you know if you should go to work? You can start by asking yourself some questions:

- Is working outside of the home necessary right now?
- What does my husband think about it?
- Is this God's will?
- Have I truly prayed for guidance?
- How much time will I spend away from home?
- Will I be available to my husband?
- Will I know my children's hearts and be able to nurture them?
- Is the financial gain worth the sacrifice?

Then, examine your heart. Why am I working?

- Is it to be an independent woman with "my own money"?
- Is it because I don't trust my husband or the Lord to provide?
- So my degree will not go to waste?
- I don't want to throw away my career.
- So I will not "lose myself."
- Being with kids all day is difficult.
- I can't sit in the house all day.
- My family and friends expect me to work.
- I don't want to disappoint my employer or coworkers.
- I want to feel purpose.

If you are working or considering working, these are some very difficult questions that you may not be ready to answer. That is okay. If you desire the Lord's will for your life, He will lead you. You must trust him. God has created you with great purpose, and if you are obedient, He will bring you into the fullness of your purpose, in his timing. Every talent, ability, and passion that he put in you will be brought out for His use. All of the skills, knowledge, and experience that you gain will play into what He wants you to do. However, if you try to bring your own dreams to fruition, you will cheat yourself out of great blessings.

Now, the Lord most certainly will accomplish His purposes in all things, but you decide whether you are on the side of victory or regret. If you are worried about making ends meet, worry no more. The Lord will make a way. If you decide to leave or turn down a job so that you can be more available to your family, surely He will provide. I know this to be true.

I started culinary school when our oldest daughter was just three months old. Toward the end of the program, I began working at a large catering company as a summer intern. They liked my work, so I was hired in as an employee. We would do huge wedding parties, Bar Mitzvahs, and various on-site events. Some weeks I would be working at three different locations. Sometimes I would work fourteen-hour shifts and still have to keep up with school work, and take care of my family. It was rough at times, but overall a lot of fun. While working, I became pregnant with our second child. Our oldest child was two years old. I was sick for four full months. The nausea was constant. I hated food: the taste, the smell, the fact that I had to eat it, and that I had to work with it every day.

I was so sick that I just wanted to live in my bed. When it was time for me to go to work, my husband and daughter would be cuddled up watching TV, and I wanted nothing more than to just be with them. I would cry before I left home, and again in the car before going in. Whereas before, I was talkative and silly in the kitchen, I became quiet and straight-faced. I worked. I left. After seeing me cry so many times, my husband got fed up. "Why are you working, then?" he said. Kardell had never influenced me to work. He was not against it. He just never expected me to have income. Every time I would cry, he would say, "Well, quit"; then I would say, "I don't want to"; and he would say, "then stop crying." Our household was not dependent on my income. It was pretty much a bonus. Why then, was I stretching myself during a difficult pregnancy?

It was because I did not want to lose my sense of accomplishment. I did not want to throw away my career, and I did not want to disappoint my boss and my co-workers. They were depending on me. Who would take my place? How would things work out? When would I go back? I grew weary of trying to silently throw up in the employee bathroom. My energy was quite low because I was not taking in enough food. I was afraid to quit, so I just took maternity leave. I felt so free. Well, for a little while, at least.

When I came home, it was a new world. It was the first time that I had been at home with my daughter every day since she was a newborn. The degree program that I chose was extremely demanding. Besides completing general study requirements, the core kitchen classes were like a full time job. We had to run campus restaurants, as well as put on buffets and dinner events. One class could be 6 hours. I also worked at a café on campus.

Back at home, it was just me and my daughter. I would clean the house from top to bottom, daily. I would do something fun with her, then prepare dinner. My days were so mundane; so repetitive. On top of that, Zahria was a strong-willed child who never slept. I felt trapped. I would try to call someone to talk and they would be at work. Then

I felt embarrassed that I called because I felt as though I should have been, too. Then there was the money challenge.

When I was working, I was used to controlling money. Kardell always gave me the freedom to do as I pleased with what I earned. He didn't even expect me to contribute. However, I do not believe in having separate finances in marriage, so I always used the money for the benefit of the household. After my last check, I had to ask my husband for money if I needed anything. I would tell him, "I need $10." "For what?" he would ask. I would say, "what does it matter? Can I have it or not?" This was very humbling for me. I was not too proud to ask him for money, but I was frustrated that I now had to check-in when I wanted to buy a stick of deodorant. To be clear, he never withheld anything from me and always gave freely. He just had to learn to give me discretionary money so that I would not feel like a little kid getting permission for every purchase.

Before leaving the workplace, it was easy for me to deny service requests from my husband. If he wanted sex or something to eat, I could legitimately express how tired I was from school and work. I mean, who wouldn't understand that? When I became a housewife, I knew that there was no excuse for me to not serve my household fully. Truth be told, there was no excuse while I was working.

My first responsibility was to my family. I realized that work was way easier than staying home. I wanted to go back to escape the difficult assignment. With a newborn and a toddler, going back would require much too great of a sacrifice. It just was not worth it.

A couple years in, I was getting the hang of staying at home and no longer entertained the idea of returning to work. However, I did struggle with feeling unfulfilled. At twenty-three, I was already married with two kids. Everyone on social media looked happy, successful, and free. People kept asking me what my career plans were, and when I would start the business that I always wanted. I felt like a failure.

By the grace of God, I pressed past those feelings and embraced my role even more. The turning point of my role as a housewife was when I decided to find out what the bible said about what a good wife and mother did. I read Proverbs 31:10-31. I had read it before in the past, but this time I wrote down what each verse meant and how it applied in the life of a woman in my day and culture. After I got a clear understanding of what I was supposed to do, I began to work toward it. My new goal was to become a virtuous woman. Here is what I gathered:

10 Who can find a virtuous woman? for her price is far above rubies.	A virtuous woman is rare and extremely valuable.
11 The heart of her husband doth safely trust in her, so that he shall have no need of spoil.	Her husband is able to trust her. She helps him move forward.
12 She will do him good and not evil all the days of her life.	She devotes her life to serving him in love. She is faithful and loyal.
13 She seeketh wool, and flax, and worketh willingly with her hands.	She is creative and uses raw materials to make things.
14 She is like the merchants' ships; she bringeth her food from afar.	She goes through a lot to produce one item.
15 She riseth also while it is yet night, and giveth meat to her household, and a portion to her maidens.	She anticipates the needs of her family. She is always prepared.

¹⁶ *She considereth a field, and buyeth it: with the fruit of her hands she planteth a vineyard.*	She creates ways to bring resources into the house.
¹⁷ *She girdeth her loins with strength, and strengtheneth her arms.*	She is physically strong. She keeps herself strong and sharp by working.
¹⁸ *She perceiveth that her merchandise is good: her candle goeth not out by night.*	She knows that she has a great product or service that people want to buy. She doesn't rest until her job is done.
¹⁹ *She layeth her hands to the spindle, and her hands hold the distaff.*	She is skilled with hand work.
²⁰ *She stretcheth out her hand to the poor; yea, she reacheth forth her hands to the needy.*	She is generous to those in need.
²¹ *She is not afraid of the snow for her household: for all her household are clothed with scarlet.*	She is not worried about hard times. She is prepared.
²² *She maketh herself coverings of tapestry; her clothing is silk and purple.*	She beautifully decorates her home. She dresses herself nicely.
²³ *Her husband is known in the gates, when he sitteth among the elders of the land.*	Her husband is well known. She makes him look good.

²⁴ *She maketh fine linen, and selleth it; and delivereth girdles unto the merchant.*	She uses her skills to bring money into the household.
²⁵ *Strength and honor are her clothing; and she shall rejoice in time to come.*	She is honorable. Her future is bright.
²⁶ *She openeth her mouth with wisdom; and in her tongue is the law of kindness.*	She speaks wisdom and kindness to build up her household.
²⁷ *She looketh well to the ways of her household, and eateth not the bread of idleness.*	She is very productive and constantly tending to the needs of the household.
²⁸ *Her children arise up, and call her blessed; her husband also, and he praiseth her.*	Her husband and children know how valuable she is.
²⁹ *Many daughters have done virtuously, but thou excellest them all.*	She is an exceptional woman.
³⁰ *Favour is deceitful, and beauty is vain: but a woman that feareth the Lord, she shall be praised.*	Most importantly, she fears the lord.
³¹ *Give her of the fruit of her hands; and let her own works praise her in the gates.*	Her hard work will pay off and she will be greatly praised.

Overall, the virtuous woman is a servant dedicated to her household. She works hard to give her family what they need. She is motivated by love. This passage of scripture is an awesome goal to work toward.

Once I had an idea of what I should do as a wife and mother, it changed my whole mindset. I was on a mission. It was not enough for me to just "do my job." I wanted to excel at it. I went from just completing tasks to managing a household. I began to see that household management was so much more than what society says.

It is not enough to just cook meals. We must prepare food that sustains the health of our family, and also food that is pleasing to the palate. We can feed our children, bathe them, and even help them with homework. However, if we do not pursue their hearts, cultivate their talents, and continually feed them the word of God as much as we do food, then I am sorry to say that we are simply babysitting. Our husbands need more than food and sex. They need genuine encouragement, constant intercessory prayer, and a woman of faith who can see God's great calling on His life, despite his short comings. These are just a few aspects of managing a household, and these alone require great mental, emotional, and spiritual stamina.

Once I was able to grasp these concepts, I began to realize that I was not ready to return to work. There was way too much to do. I had invested my soul into my household and there was no way that I was going to disrupt what was being built. I was fully committed, but I was still holding fast to my dreams that seemed so foggy.

For the single mothers: be encouraged. Even though you carry a heavy burden, know that the Lord is with you. You are getting a chance to see what many women do not. That is, the full strength and resilience that is within. Although I am married, the Lord has given me experiences that give me insight into what single mothers must endure.

My husband has always worked very long hours: twelve hour days, plus two additional hours for traveling time. Sometimes he would work seven days a week. This does not include any other places that he has to go. We joke around that he works 8 days a week. When he gets home, he falls onto his face to sleep. Sometimes he is gone so often that his return disturbs the household. The children get worked up or out of bed, and then I have to deal with the crying when he leaves again. One time he called me and said he was coming home to pick up his lunch before work, and I told him not to come into the house. "I'll put it on the porch because the last thing I need is for all of them to wake up." He laughed and said, "That's crazy." I felt like we weren't even together. I learned to cope by adopting the mindset that I have to do it all myself, and if he is able to help me, it's a bonus.

I know what it's like to go grocery shopping with four kids: an eight-year-old, a five-year-old, a two-year-old, and a newborn. You load up your vehicle, get home, have the eight-year-old unlock the door, carry the screaming newborn into the house, post the five-year-old at the door as the receiver, hand the two-year-old the bread and demand that he carries his weight, while you and the eight-year-old relay the groceries into the house. Then, while the kids put the groceries away, you waste no time pulling out pots and pans to prepare for dinner. Oh, and the baby is still in the car seat on the couch screaming; but you will be right with her as soon as you get this pot on the stove, because if the food is not cooking while you nurse, then the other kids will have to wait longer for dinner.

My husband worked the night shift for about a year. When he left for work at 9:00 p.m., guess what? I had to assume the responsibility of the guard. When I heard a sound, I had to check it out. I went to bed later because I could not sleep until everyone was still. On top of that, my two-year-old and seven-month-old would wake me up about three times a night. Then I would still have to get up very early because my husband would come home around 7:30 a.m. If I stayed in bed, then that would mean all of the children constantly coming in to talk to me.

If there was a power outage, I was in the electrical box. If a flame went out on the furnace or hot water tank, I was lighting the pilot. If there was a mouse in the house, it was all mine. One day, I was talking to my dad on the phone about the hot water tank. He was telling me what I could do to fix it. With frustration, I interrupted his instructions as it dawned on me. "Is it me or do these things only happen when Kardell is not here?" He said, "These things only happen when he is not there." Honestly, in the past four years, almost every house issue has happened when he was not home. Why do I always have to go into a dark basement, shining the light from my cell phone, and swatting spider webs?

One day I was really discouraged and having a moment. My dad called me, and by the sound of my voice, he knew something was wrong. I told him how hard everything was. I was trying to balance homeschooling four kids, and manage a home with my husband at work *all* the time. I had been thinking it for a long time, but afraid to say it out loud for fear of sounding ungrateful to the Lord. "I feel like it would be easier if I wasn't married. Besides income, I feel like a single mother." He told me to tread carefully with what I was saying. I further explained. I did not mean that I didn't want to be married anymore. What I meant was, on top of all the things that I have to do alone, I still have to serve my husband. There was just no balance. My dad didn't get it. We hung up.

The next day he called and said, "You know what? Maybe the Lord wants you to feel what it's like to be a single mother so that you can minister to them, too." This is where the hope came in. It became clear to me. All the things that I had been through in the past 5 years, all the struggles, tears, pain, and frustration was so that I could have some credibility to all mothers: single and married. If I had it to do all over again, I would, just to be able to encourage you to press on and believe that The Lord is working in your favor. "And we know that all things work together for good to them that love The Lord and are called according to his purpose (Romans 8:28)."

Chapter 2

Shop 'til you Drop?

S hopping can be fun and even therapeutic, but we have to be responsible and wise. We cannot allow our emotions to shop for us and rob our households of valuable resources. Train yourself to think, "Before I make any purchases, I must be able to justify the cost." We are supposed to be good stewards over the resources that God has given us. This means that before we purchase anything, whether a pack of gum or a new vehicle, we must do some thinking. We have needs and we have wants. They are relative to the person. You must decide honestly and wisely what you should spend money on.

We cannot allow worldly influence and companies to tell us what we need, want, or deserve. Look at their product and make your own decision about whether or not you should buy it. If you know what is right for you, then you will not need a presentation on it. If you know that it is not right for you, then you should not allow yourself to be persuaded to buy it. When considering making a purchase, ask yourself the following questions:

- Is this a need or a want?
- Can I make it myself or find an alternative?
- Can I afford it?
- Is this the right time?
- Are there any more important things to buy?
- Will this put a strain on my marriage or family?
- Is it practical?
- Will I actually use this?

- Is this a quality product?
- What did the reviews say?
- Is this the best price?
- Are there any discounts or coupons?
- How will the seller handle returns?

If you ask yourself these questions before you buy anything, you will make wise purchasing decisions. You will have greater financial peace and you will prove yourself to be a good steward over the Lord's resources. All this sounds good in text, but how will it look in real life? Let us go through a few examples.

Purchase: A new sofa

- Do I need a sofa or do I just want it?
- Can I pay for it without putting my household in a financial bind?
- Is this the right time to buy it?
- Are there any more pressing issues in the household?
- Does my husband approve of this?
- Will the Lord approve of this?
- Does this fit my current décor, or will I need to buy something else to make it work?

- How will this fit into the space?
- Is it practical for my family?
- Overall, can I justify the cost?

- What kind of materials is it made of?
- What did the reviews say?
- How much do they sell it for in other stores?
- Are there any discounts or coupons available?
- Can I negotiate the price?
- What is the policy on returns?

Purchase: Pizza for dinner

- Is this a need or a want? Am I unable to cook or do we just want pizza?
- Do we have food at home?
- Can I afford to buy a pizza?
- How have we been eating lately?
- Who has the best pizza?
- Are there any specials?

Purchase: A cute pair of shoes

- Is this a need or a want?
- Can I afford these?
- Do I need to buy these right now?
- Do I already have something that will serve the same purpose?
- How often will I wear these?
- Do I have enough storage space for these?
- Will this put a strain on the household?
- Will my husband approve? Will the Lord approve?
- Is this a quality product?
- Can I get it for less somewhere else?

After asking yourself these questions and honestly answering them, you should be able to either buy something with confidence, or walk away from it and not have regrets. Making a purchase is not just about your ability to select and procure. If you have accepted Christ as your Lord, then He is also Lord of the money that you have. It belongs to Him. So, every penny that you spend, you must be able to justify it.

If you were the owner of a company and you gave your employees discretionary funds to make purchases that would benefit the company, surely you would require that they give an account for what they did with the money. You would want to be sure that they were making financial decisions that would ultimately advance the company, and not those that were rooted in selfish gain or foolishness. If you did an audit and found that they were abusing their financial liberty, you would limit their control or even take it away altogether. You most certainly would not give them more.

> If we mismanage God's money, then He will limit what He places in our hands.
>
> The Lord gives us resources not only for ourselves but for others as well. He entrusts us to distribute blessings to His people and to the world.

It is the same in the kingdom of God. If you do not use the Lord's wisdom and practice self-control with money, you can fall into debt, allow shopping or products to become idols, or miss out on what He wants to bless you with. If we mismanage God's money, then He will limit what He places in our hands.

The Lord gives us resources not only for ourselves, but for others as well. He entrusts us to distribute blessings to

His people and to the world. Sometimes what we may think is a surplus could very well belong to someone else. If we are not in tune with the voice of the Holy Spirit, we can miss the call to action. The virtuous woman gives to the needy.

One of my spiritual gifts is giving. I absolutely love to give. Many times, I wanted to help someone in some way and could not because I had not the financial means. Countless times someone needed meals because they did not have food or had just had a baby. I found myself being blind-sided by unexpected costs. It was in my heart to do it, but I could not. The Lord gave me the wisdom to be prepared to give. I decided that instead of scrambling when I saw a need, I would anticipate it. I adopted the mindset that someone will always need something. Quite often, someone that I know needs a prepared meal. Sometimes it's because they have a new baby in the family or because someone is sick. One thing that I did to be more prepared was purchase a bulk package of foil pans with lids. I also began collecting nice recyclable bags. I usually keep extra pasta or rice in my pantry. So, when someone has a need for food, I already have some items at home and I can just go out to get a few items to make a complete meal.

Whenever I get a surplus, I pause to hear what the Holy Spirit would have me to do with it. Most of the time, it's for someone else. I may save a lot of money at the grocery store or get an unexpected check. I would have dollar signs in my eyes thinking of all the things that I could buy, then I humbly ask, "Lord what would you have me to do with this?" Shortly after, I will figure out who it is for and feel victorious that I did not hold back what the Lord sent me to give to them. One time I received an unexpected refund check from the insurance company for $900 dollars. Within twenty minutes, I had already spent that money in my mind. Then, I soberly asked the Lord what He would have me to do with it. Immediately, the Holy Spirit told me who it was for. I called the person right away and told them that the Lord told me to give them $500. It was not hard for me to part with it because I understood that it belonged to the Lord anyway. After I gave them the money, my spirit overflowed with joy.

If you are constantly seeing a need that you cannot meet, the reason could be that you have already taken the resource for yourself. We must be sensitive to the needs of others. You do not have to wait for them to ask. Pay attention. "But whoso hath this world's good, and sees that his brother have need and shutteth up the bowels of compassion from him, how dwelleth the love of God in him (1 John 3:17)?" Those who have the gift of giving will be driven to give. We constantly think about giving to people. Those who do not possess the gift have to practice giving because they don't have the drive. Giving may not be your spiritual gift, but it is your spiritual responsibility. No one is exempt.

At one time in my life, I felt like we never had enough food. It seemed like we were always barely getting by. I cried out saying, "Lord! If you won't give me more money, then give me the wisdom to work with what I have." Immediately, the Holy Spirit directed my attention to a bag of beans that had been sitting on the top shelf of my cupboard for who knows how long. "Why did I buy those?" I thought to myself. We don't even eat beans. Well, we ate beans that night. I cooked those beans to the glory of God. After I used up what I had, the Lord sent me more.

"Oh fear the Lord, ye his saints: for there is no want in Him. The young lions do lack, and suffer hunger: but they that seek the Lord shall not want any good thing (Psalms 34:9-10)." God's word is truth. There is no lack in Him. So, if we feel like we do not have enough, we need to examine ourselves. Either we are mismanaging what He has given us, or maybe we are not grateful for what He has provided. God promised us that we will not lack what we need, but he did not promise that we would always have the most desirable thing. I was whining because I did not have a steak dinner. I was not entitled to that. Whether I am eating a rib-eye or legumes, He is Jehovah Jireh; God my Provider, and I should receive whatsoever He sets before me with thanksgiving.

The Lord revealed to me that all the times that I asked for more money for groceries, I was asking for the wrong thing. Why would he give me extra money when I was handling it foolishly anyway? I had many wasteful habits that made it appear that I did not have enough. That was a huge turning point in my life as a household manager. I began to seek godly knowledge and wisdom on everything that I was doing, instead of just "winging it." In the following years, the Lord gave me a lot of wisdom for grocery shopping. Who knew grocery shopping was so deep? Here are some tips:

Budget

Choose how often you will shop and stick with it. Shopping frequencies will vary from household to household. Assess your need and determine what would be most convenient. You may want to shop once a week or every two weeks. You could also purchase non-perishables monthly, and then replenish the perishable foods weekly or bi-weekly. Make a reasonable estimate of how much money it will take to buy enough groceries to last until the next shopping date. This budget can also include household items such as toiletries and cleaning products.

The Godly Household Manager

Take Inventory

See what items you already have. A good household manager knows what is in the home. It is your job to know how many rolls of tissue are left and how much milk there is. You take inventory so you will not buy something that you do not need or forget something that you do need. If your budget is $300 and you spend all of it, only to arrive home to realize that you forgot the diapers, you would have to go back. You would spend more money and you would waste time.

See what food items you already have. Is there an extra box of pasta from last week? Do you have a full stalk of celery leftover of which you removed 1 rib for a chicken salad recipe? If that be the case then, whatever you put on the meal list needs to include pasta and celery.

Check Sales

After you take inventory, check out the sales paper. See what you can get for a low price. Pull together coupons that will save you money on the items that will be helpful. Coupons are great, but I would not advise one to take up the task of "couponing." Couponing is time consuming and they mostly offer deals on food items that are processed. Also, we want to save money on what we have already decided that we need. We do not need a dollar off of a product that we otherwise would never buy. Remember not to allow people to tell you what you need. Do not be fooled into thinking that manufacturers want to save you money. Coupons are a price negotiation. You won't buy it for $3.50? How about $2.75? If you were already going to buy it, you saved $0.75. If you only bought it because of the coupon, you spent $2.75. The purpose was to get you to buy.

Check your calendar

How many days do you need to have meals for? Will you be home on the weekend? Are you going out to dinner? Count how many days you will actually need meals. If you buy food to prepare meals for fourteen days but you only needed ten meals, then you will have money tied up in your refrigerator. Say, for instance, that week you are going out to a restaurant for dinner. You could have saved the extra money spent on groceries to go toward the restaurant bill. Also, if you bought more food than you needed, some of it may spoil. Doing a meal forecast can save you a significant amount of money

Make a Menu

After you have established a budget, checked inventory and your calendar, it is time to make a menu. Choose what meals will be prepared based on your budget, schedule, your recent diet, and perishability.

You have to prepare meals that fit your budget. If it's a tight week because you have to buy a birthday gift for a kid's party, then you need to think of meals that will be inexpensive. You can find creative ways to bring cost down and still have desirable foods. It's all about balance.

Make meals with common ingredients to maximize use. If you buy avocados, cilantro, and tomatoes for Taco Tuesday, but you won't use it all, then you could have Nacho Wednesday to justify buying the ingredients. If your hardworking husband asks for steak, get the steak; but the next day you may have to make potato soup. As much as possible, cut out processed foods. They are unhealthy, they don't last long, and they are expensive. Make things from scratch. If you are not good at it, learn and practice. Saving money means doing the extra work.

Think of your family's recent diet. Have we been eating too heavily: too many fats or too much sugar? Make meals that will bring balance. Think about your week ahead. If you will be pressed for time, plan for meals that you can prepare quickly or in advance. You do not always have to resort to processed dinners that are high in sodium and contain questionable ingredients. You can even make homemade frozen dinners.

The slow cooker is also a great tool to make meal preparation easier. If you do not think ahead, you may buy meals that you don't have time to cook. Then you will probably end up getting take-out. It's ok to have take-out, but it should be because you want it and not because you have no other options due to lack of planning.

Some foods are more perishable than others. How do you buy produce two weeks in advance without it going bad? Here is what you do. Purposely plan to make some foods with perishable items and other foods with non-perishable items. For example, in the first few days, make the Mexican food so that you can use up those perishable ingredients first. Toward the end of the week or the next week, make foods that are less perishable like beef stew with frozen mixed vegetables, or spaghetti. This method of planning will cut down on waste. If you have ever found a bag of liquefied produce that you didn't get a chance to use, then you know what I mean.

Before the Lord taught me how to shop, I wasted a lot of food. If I wrote a grocery list, it wasn't exhaustive; I just wrote a few ideas. My method was to go into the store and buy what looked good. I would buy produce that I had no plans for. Every week, I would throw away produce that I didn't use. I would buy a gallon of milk but we never could finish it. I would buy a loaf of bread and we would eat half of it. Yet, I thought that we didn't have enough. I thought grocery prices were too high.

The Ingredient List

Now you can make your grocery list. Go through each menu item and mentally walk through the preparation. Write down all the things that you need to buy. You have already done inventory, so you know what you already have. Break your list into six categories: meat, produce, dairy, grocery, household items, and miscellaneous. Organize each category according to the layout of the store. With this system, you can shop in an organized way without having to double back to the produce section five times. Also, if you are shopping at a specialty store such as a meat market, you do not want to be confused by a list that has produce on it. With an organized list, you can walk into the store with purpose, and walk out with what you planned to buy and not what you felt like buying once you got there.

Shopping

Keep track of your cost in your mind. When you get to the check out, you should not be over budget. If it's not on your list, keep it moving. Be strong because those companies will be trying to sell to you. "New!"; "No, thank you." "Would you like a sample?"; "Sure, but I'm not buying." "Limited time offer?"; "Maybe, next time." Now there are times when it is appropriate to make adjustments. If you see a very low price on chicken breast, swap out a meal, and change the menu. If what you planned for costs more than what you are willing to pay, change it. Maybe you will decide to go over budget in the store. If you do, it should be a sober decision and not be because of carelessness.

Never shop without a list. You will spend more money, forget some things, and then have to go back and spend even more money. You must be purposeful about shopping. I remember a time when my older sister and I were grocery shopping together. She picked up a cute little pack of miniature glass bottles of Coca-Cola. They were adorable. We were saying, "aww." She grabbed one and said to me, "Are you getting one?" I said, "No." She said, "Why not?" "Because it's not on my list," I said. She replied, "Do you ever get anything that's not on your list?" "Not really," I said. We both laughed. Granted, there are actually times when I will get something that's not on my list. I know that I will see something that I like or want to try, or my husband may call and ask for something specific. I anticipate this so I do not go over budget.

Most of the time, I shop with my kids. They are there to learn and to help, not to badger and beg. I always let them have input on the list. I am not afraid of the cereal or cookie aisle because they know that mama will not give in. No amount of begging will get me to *feel* a purchase. As a matter of fact, they don't even ask because they know that they don't have a chance. Not because I am mean, but because I am here with a goal and a purpose: to select and procure, *not* to shop 'til I drop. After checking out, I am never over my budget. It took time and practice for me to be that accurate. It is definitely possible.

We must look at shopping for our household similar to the way we would view shopping for a business. Remove the emotion and develop solid order. There should be a recognizable pattern. Shopping can be fun to do, but we cannot allow it to become an idol in our lives. Shopping can be overwhelming and you may hate it, but that is not an excuse to approach it without a plan. The Lord provides all of our needs. His word tells us, there is no lack in Him. If we think that we are lacking something, the lack is in our own trust, obedience, or wisdom. There is nothing wrong with buying things that we want, but we must be sure that our desires are coming from a godly heart. There must be balance. We have to be able to justify the cost.

Chapter 3

The Cook

I knew since 8th grade that I wanted to be chef and the Lord blessed me to achieve that dream. Cooking is my passion. I never get tired of it. It is the highlight of my day. I do, however, understand that for many women, this can be a laborious task or an area of weakness. Either way, we must rise to the challenge of providing nutrition to keep our families healthy. Cooking is also a necessary skill to teach children, and a great way to make memories and strengthen bonds.

In my generation, it is common for women not to know much about cooking. Some even boast about not knowing how to boil water. Our mothers were career women. They put away their aprons and became consumers. They outsourced their jobs as home cooks to Betty Crocker and McDonald's. As a result, many millennial women struggle to prepare descent meals for their families. All these years later, we see the effects of being a consumer in the area of prepared meals. Obesity, cancers, diabetes, and hear disease are the consequences of too many shortcuts. Let us turn away from unhealthy convenience foods and get back to what grandma and great grandma did: spend time cooking meals from scratch for the family.

So, your mother worked a full time job and did not get a chance to teach you how to cook. Got it. Now it's time to learn. Don't you tell one more person, "I'm not a good cook." You are a home manager, and home managers do not say, "I can't." They find out how. So tell them, "I am currently improving my cooking skills through trial and error." Don't get mad at your husband because he told you that the chicken breast was dry. Listen to the critiques and make adjustments accordingly. We are living in an era of an information explosion. We can find out anything we want to know in the form of books, web pages, and videos. Many of which are free. Take advantage. Own your job. I digress.

Food Safety

Handwashing is crucial in the kitchen. The risk of food-borne illness is significantly reduced when we make hand-washing a frequent routine. If you think that this sounds basic and can't believe that I am mentioning this, you are off to a great start.

Your hands harbor many pathogens that can be transferred to food. Under proper conditions, those pathogens can grow exponentially, doubling every twenty minutes. So a single bacterial cell can grow to a colony of one billion in ten hours, and we know that there will be much more than a single cell. You do not want to be the "Typhoid Mary" of your household. You should wash your hands thoroughly with hot, soapy water before you begin cooking; and after touching raw meat, your body, or anything else that could harbor harmful bacteria.

Bacteria are everywhere and on everything. Our best defense against bacterial growth is controlling their environment. If conditions are not ideal for harmful microorganisms to flourish, then they cannot grow to levels great enough to make us sick. Some bacteria that cause common food-borne illnesses include Salmonella *typhi*, Esherichia *coli* (E.Coli), and Listeria *monocytogenes*. They can reproduce to levels large enough to cause you a night hanging over the toilet or even death. In order for these pathogens to thrive, they need: Food, Acidity, Time, Temperature, Oxygen, and Moisture. The National Restaurant Association's ServSafe course book calls this "FAT TOM."

Food

Bacteria are definitely on your food when you get it home. It is naturally in the soil that produce grows in and on animals that we use for meats. More bacteria can be introduced during the processes of harvesting, butchering, transporting, and setting on display at your local grocery store. Bacteria can grow on any food, but some foods have the potential to be especially hazardous. Foods rich in protein are ideal for bacteria because protein is their food source. Some of the ideal food sources include: meats, fish, shellfish, eggs, milk products tofu, baked potatoes and cooked rice, beans, and vegetables. Some foods are potentially hazardous because the soil that they grow in naturally contains harmful bacteria. These foods include melons, which can contain Listeria monocytogenes; and potatoes and garlic, which can contain Clostridium botulinum. Listeria is extremely dangerous in that it can go undetected for thirty days, it has the highest fatality rate, and it can cross the uterine wall, causing pregnant women to miscarry. Clostridium botulinum produces a toxin that causes botulism. Botulism is very deadly. It affects the nervous system and can cause paralysis. Without treatment, a person will most likely die.

Acidity

Microorganisms grow best in a neutral to slightly acidic environment. A pH of about 7.5 to 4.6. This is the pH of most foods, so bacteria can thrive on almost all foods. Highly acidic foods, like lemons; and highly alkaline foods, such as crackers, are not a high risk.

Time

Bacteria needs time to grow. Under the best conditions, the more time it has, the greater the risk. This is why we should not leave food sitting out for too long.

Temperature

Temperature is our best way to control microorganisms. We refrigerate foods at (40°) to slow down the growth rate and we cook foods to kill the bacteria. During the cooking process, bacteria begins to die at (140°). So, between 40 and 140 is what is called the "temperature danger zone." This is the stage at which growth is rapid. This is meat sitting on your counter for eight hours. This is dinner sitting on the stove for two hours. The best defense against food-borne pathogens is to not let them grow.

Oxygen

Most bacteria need oxygen to live. However, there is a group of bacteria that prefer anaerobic environments; these are usually the most dangerous strains. Clostridium botulinum is one of them.

Moisture

Bacteria need a moist environment to thrive. Foods with high water content are an ideal breeding ground. Produce with the skin intact is protected.

Now, that we have food safety awareness, let's get to it. A cook is one who does just that. Cook. We have been taught to be consumers. You can purchase absolutely any food item mostly done, if not completely done. The message that is being sent is: "You cannot do this. Just buy our product" or "You don't have the time for this." We must not allow the sellers to tell us what we need and want. We must make informed decisions about what products we will use to prepare food. Some of us have never seen certain food items prepared, so we really don't know if it is difficult to prepare from scratch. One example of such a product is spaghetti sauce. There are so many different brands and recipes available on the shelf. Who has time to make spaghetti sauce from scratch anyway? Jars of spaghetti sauce were my friends. As my family grew, I needed to buy more than one jar, so the cost became uncomfortable for me. I began to wonder, "How hard could it be?"

When thinking of homemade pasta sauce, some of us imagine an old Italian lady stirring a pot of sauce made from perfectly ripened tomatoes that she picked from her own garden, along with some herbs that you could never find at your store. She stirs this sauce for hours and at dinner time, she has just enough to pour over each pasta portion for her family. Please! I found a basic recipe and started trial and error from there. I improved each time, and when I got it down, I made huge batches and froze it. The cost difference is significant, and I know exactly what is and is not in my sauce.

Please do not roll your eyes at the above paragraph thinking that I have an unrealistic idea of the average woman cooking in this day. I do believe in balance. Finished products most certainly do have their place. However, the decision cannot be based solely on one factor. It may be faster, but is it healthy? It may be convenient, but is it economical? Surely, we all need to cut a corner every now and again, but you cannot cut corners on *everything* all the time. I absolutely love to cook and try my best to keep my family healthy, but sometimes I just have to find the heathiest frozen meal that I can. Or, I will call my husband and say, "I can't cook. Will you pick something up?" Convenience food should not be the norm for us. It is expensive; high in fats, sugars, and sodium; and full of substances that are harmful to our bodies.

> The health of the family ultimately lies in the hands of the cook.

I like to make a wide variety of dishes and I don't "stay away" from any particular foods. However, because I prepare all of the meals, it is my responsibility to make sure my family is healthy. The health of the family ultimately lies in the hands of the cook. I do not ascribe to any particular diet plan or fad, I just do the best that I can with what I have and what I know. As I learn more, I make changes accordingly and I try to maintain balance.

If around holiday times we eat a lot of rich food, the next week we will have light foods like soups, salads, and meatless meals. Overall, I watch our fat, sugar, and salt intake, and make sure that we are taking in proper nutrients through produce. I once had a problem getting my kids to drink water, so I just stopped buying any kind of sweetened beverages. I no longer have that problem. I saved some money, too. I will buy lemonade or juice on special occasions or for guests.

I keep a heavy arsenal of snacks for my kids, but I try to keep it as healthy as possible. I give them homemade muffins; raisins; homemade popcorn; grapefruit; carrots and celery; cheese; hummus and pita; or yogurt with homemade granola. I try to change it up often. Homemade snacks made with wholesome ingredients are healthier and cost way less money, too.

Even if you are an extremely busy person, you can still cook healthy foods for your family. The mind that the Lord gave to the woman is awesome. He made us so creative and we are able to make things happen. If you know that your family is not eating well, make the changes now. I'm not telling you to go into your kitchen and toss all of your food, but take steps toward a better diet. Start with what you know and build from there. Switch out one product at a time and week by week. It's a journey.

Many people ask me in awe, how I make certain foods. I may have a family gathering or post a picture on social media. I never want people to think that I do kitchen magic. My cooking skills come by trial and error. I make something. Sometimes it's good. Sometimes it's not and my family has no problem telling me. "Mama, this food is not good," is what my six-year-old, Zoey, might say. "Don't make that again," my husband has said a few times. I ask them what they don't like so that I can make a mental note for improvements the next time. If it has potential, I work on it until it is great. Then I post a picture on Facebook and people think it's just fabulous. The point is that great cooks are not born; they are made. If your cooking skills are minimal, then improve. Watch cooking shows, search for recipes online, read food magazines. Call your grandma. Do something! Do not cheat your family and yourself out of a lifetime of good home cooked meals.

Another great reason to cook at home is so that you can to teach your children. This is a basic, yet essential, life skill. They will learn a lot by watching you, and even more when they help. If they can hold a toy, they can hold a spatula. You do not have to be a great cook. You all can practice together. It's also a great opportunity to spend quality time. When you have a full life, it can be difficult to carve out quality time. Cooking together can definitely count as that.

At my house, dinner time can be very stressful. The kids seem to be at their peak of energy and my husband may not be home yet. It is a challenge to prepare a meal and try to keep kids in line. I have found it quite helpful to invite all of them into the kitchen and give each one a task. Things get knocked over, they make mistakes, but the reward is twofold: time together and learning a new skill.

There are seasons in our lives where it seems that you spend more time out of the house than in. We have to take the kids to school, practices, appointments, playdates, and birthday parties, and even still get ourselves to work, meetings, the grocery store, or church commitments. If you have ever spent an entire day driving, you know what I mean. In these seasons, we can really lose focus on properly nourishing the body. We may turn to junk food for snacks and fast food for meals. It does not have to be this way. If we plan ahead, we can eat a balanced diet even on-the-go.

What is the first thing that comes to mind when thinking about lunches and snacks for American kids? Processed meats and cheeses, bleach wheat products, salty snacks, and sugary beverages. Right? If you have found yourself trapped in this cultural habit, now is the time to get out. We must re-train our brains. The goal is to provide our families with foods that will support the body's functions. God has given us a wide variety of foods to choose from.

Our children's lunches do not have to look like everyone else's. As long as it is nourishing and they like it, then send it. What exactly do I mean? Think outside of the box. If your kid liked that chick pea salad that you made the other day, send it for lunch. Give them sugar peas and carrots. Chicken wraps or chopped meat from home. Search the web for healthy lunch ideas.

We live in a culture where we say things like "kid friendly" foods. We assume what kids will and will not eat. Make no mistake about it: your children get their definition of food and their eating habits from you. If you want to change what your children call food, simply redefine it. Don't be afraid or ashamed to tell your kids that you need to make some changes. Countless times, I had to tell my kids that we would no longer be buying or eating a particular item. They were upset initially, but then they got over it. Now, they don't get upset at all because they desire health for themselves. When I changed my definition of food, the household definition of food changed as well.

I remember as a kid, I wanted to have a lunch just like the rest of the kids. I wanted to have stacks of meat, cheese, and crackers in a little tray, a juice pouch, and something sweet. I remember one day, my mother took the roast from dinner and made me a sandwich. I was so embarrassed. I hid the sandwich under the lunch table and took bites when no one was looking. I didn't want a leftovers sandwich. I wanted to have a cool lunch with jokes on the back and a maze to complete while eating. I wanted to eat like everyone else. Now that I am older, I realize that she sent me a great lunch.

Your children may eat school lunch and you may not have the means to prepare their lunch at home. If the school is serving a nutritious lunch, then you are covered. If they are serving anything like what I was eating in Detroit Public Schools in 1995, then you must take action. It is not the will of God that our kids eat unhealthy food. You must ask Him for more wisdom. He will show you just what to do.

Kids need snacks in between meals, but we must not make snacks synonymous with junk food. Do I ever feed my kids junk food? Absolutely! Who doesn't want some cheesy, salty stuff or a donut sometimes? I limit those foods and choose high quality products that do not contain artificial ingredients. Most of the time I make it myself. When they think of a snack, I want them to think of things like tangerines, raw sugar peas, popcorn, or peanut butter. When their bodies are trained to eat healthy whole foods, then junk food, though tasty, will not satisfy them.

Before I knew any better, I fed my family foods with harmful ingredients all the time. My husband was the skinny guy who could eat anything and burn it off. When we changed our diets, our bodies changed, and so did our taste buds. Whenever we tried to go back to eating bad foods, we would regret it. When my husband is leaving the house, I always tell him to eat before he leaves or take food with him. He always says, "I'll be okay." Then if he gets hungry and resorts to fast food, he gets sick.

At first I was unsure of how strict I should be with my kids and their diet. I didn't want to be at birthday parties asking if the cake icing was made with real butter or hydrogenated fat. I found balance by maintaining a consistent clean diet at home and allowing them to have other things when they are out. Sometimes when they eat the foods that they aren't used to, they get sick. I figure, eventually they will realize that the effect the foods have on their bodies is not worth the temporary pleasure that they had chewing it. One day they will say, "no, thank you."

Feeding your husband well is very important. A married man should not have to cook because his wife refuses. If a man is doing what God called Him to do and providing for the household, then you, the wife, need to do what God called you to do and be a helper. In this context, you ought to help him by preparing food. If your husband is not being the provider that God called him to be, then you better cook his food to the glory of God and pray that he starts providing, because you still have to serve him and serve him well. Many women have full schedules that include full-time jobs and/or school. They should still prepare meals. The first responsibility is the home. If your husband enjoys cooking or is willing to cook often, then that is a great bonus. If not, you cannot be mad at him because it's not what the Lord called a husband do to. However, the bible commands that husbands love their wives. Sometimes loving the wife means cooking dinner because she is tired. Still, it is not the man's responsibility. The woman is the help meet. Now, call me old-fashioned, but I believe that this is the way that it is supposed to be, and so did the rest of the world until Lady Lib "set women free."

When I was working outside of the home, I still would come straight in and start cooking for my family. Some days my husband would be off and home all day, but still would not cook. He never demanded that I cook and if I didn't, he wouldn't complain. He was always willing to go pick up food, but he just did not want to cook. The very few times that he did cook, he made meat with no sides. He also had no problem with me working or not working because it was simply not my job to provide. I really had no basis to be upset with him. I would be tired, but my first responsibility was in the home. Thankfully, he is now beginning to enjoy cooking.

When Kardell was working a twelve-hour day shift, he would usually go in around 5:00 a.m. and get off at 5:00 p.m. I would send him a lunch, but he would text me from work at noon and say that he was starving. When my husband says that he is hungry, I feel like my job is not done. After getting so many texts like that, I decided that I would make sure I sent him plenty of food.

I first asked him how many times a day he normally ate. Then I asked him what kinds of foods he needed. He told me that he needed breakfast, a full meal, then snacks. I know that some really wise women wake up with their husbands and make breakfast and send them away with a lunch and a kiss. Perhaps, I will be able to do that when I no longer do laundry after 9:00 p.m., have a nursing infant that wakes up three times a night, and have to get up with the rest of the kids early in the morning.

He would leave for work at 4:00 a.m. Cereal is not a sufficient breakfast for a man that does physical labor or even a man who does no labor. He would burn that off during the car ride. Again, I am not getting out of bed. The Lord gave me wisdom on how to give him a good breakfast without having to get up. I started making sausage and spinach omelets. I cooked a large batch of sausage and spinach, portioned it out into individual sandwich bags and froze it. Before going to bed, I would cook the egg portion of the omelet, put it on a plate, place the frozen sausage and spinach mixture on it, sprinkle shredded cheese, and then fold the egg. When he woke up, he would put the plate in the microwave for 1 minute and it would be hot and cheesy as if I had just made it. So, there, he had a nutritious homemade breakfast that would keep him full at least half way until his first break. I would send him last night's dinner for lunch, as well as snacks like homemade yogurt parfaits, smoothies, nuts, and beef jerky.

I am blessed to have a husband that places no demands on me. He is very cool and laid back. If I don't fix him anything to eat, he won't fuss. I make a much bigger deal out of his lunch than even he does. I don't want to give the impression that I am perfect in this area (nor any other), because I am not. There are times when I just cannot do it. I may be exhausted, sick with pregnancy, or just forget. One thing that I can tell you is that it is in my heart to feed him well, so grace makes up for the rest. He may have to eat fast food or go hungry, but I will make up for it and try to do better.

Sometimes if I drop the ball, he will say "I'll be alright" or I'll get something." There were times when I said "just give me five more minutes and it will be ready." It's the love of God that drives me to go above that which is asked of me. It definitely was not in me before.

I used to only make his lunch as long as he stayed in favor with me. I have since graduated to maturity. The scripture says in 1 Corinthians 10:31, "Whether therefore you eat or drink, or whatsoever ye do, do it all to the glory of God." When you work to the glory of God, another person's actions will not discourage your effort. When a man pulls out his lunch at work, people should see a spread and call him blessed, not a baloney sandwich and call him single.

Establishing mealtimes will help maintain order in your house and ensure that food is not being consumed frivolously. Decide how many times you want to have a meal and set the times. Children should only be able to eat at these established times. This will relieve the stress that comes along with a child saying that they are hungry all the time.

When we only had one child, we had breakfast, lunch, and dinner, and in addition to that, we fed her whenever she said she was hungry. It wasn't a problem until we had our second child. It was like I was getting something to eat for someone every twenty minutes. I got fed up and put a stop to it. I established five meal times: breakfast, snack, lunch, snack, and dinner. Then I made it clear that they would not eat a crumb outside of these times. I always arrange dinner time around Kardell's schedule because he is the man of the house. Even at the times when he worked afternoons and had to be at work at five o'clock, I had dinner ready at three in the afternoon, which was very difficult.

Establishing mealtimes makes it easy to keep track of how much food you actually need. For example, I usually give my kids muffins for a snack at 10:30 a.m. during the week. So, when I multiply one muffin per kid, per day by five days, I know exactly how many muffins I need. Then, I know how many batches I need to make, and thus, how much of the ingredients I need. This organization allows me to get exactly what I need from the store so that I don't have to return before the next shopping date. When children know that they can only eat at specific times, they are more likely to eat when food is available.

Food is important in the home for a few reasons. Of course, it keeps us alive, but it also gives us many opportunities to sit down and enjoy something together. We make memories together and teach our children an important life skill: cooking. Become a great cook by faith.

Chapter 4

One Flesh

Marriage is a very sacred institution that has been ordained by God. The Lord brings together two human beings who He made in His image: complex individually, and even more so together. Sin added to those complexities causes confusion. Marriage is so profound that it takes a lifetime of matrimony for us to truly understand God's purpose for marriage in the earth, as well as His purpose for our specific unions.

There is an abundance of marital advice available. People have different opinions about how to please your mate and how to keep your marriage together. I think that the best way to map out marriage is on a macro level, as opposed to a micro level. There are three main principles to help guide and grow your marriage to the glory of God: Cleave, Serve, and Pray.

Cleave

In the book of Genesis, The Lord says, "Therefore shall a man leave his father and mother, and shall cleave unto his wife: and they shall become one flesh." On the day that we are married, we are joined together, but we 'become one' over the course of our marriage. God created us as spirits with souls, all wrapped in flesh. In order to truly 'become one,' we must understand God's design, as well as the damage done after the fall of the creation.

The body

The first level that we are joined on is the physical level. First and most importantly, the marriage is consummated by the joining together of our bodies through sexual intimacy. Our bodies belong to one another to fulfill pleasure and provide comfort. We need to be hugged, kissed, and touched. The more that we feel each other and engage in sexual intercourse, the stronger our bond will be.

Our bodies belong to each other and God put it in us to be attracted to one another. Wives should keep themselves looking attractive to their husbands. I have heard people say that you should get fully dressed everyday so you can look as good as the women that your husband sees all day. I've also heard that "men are visual beings; they want something good to look at." This is true, but the problem lies in what is being defined as attractive. Looking good cannot be limited to fancy clothes and make up.

I once heard someone say that even if you stay home, you should get dressed as if you are leaving. I tried it out and I found it to be impractical. I believe you should be dressed for the job. When I wash dishes, I get my shirt wet every time. Sometimes I may sit on the floor to change a diaper or Zahna may put her peanut-butter hands on my pants. Now, why would I want to be wearing my "time-to-go clothes," as my kids call them?

I usually put on active wear. I keep my hair done and put on scented lotions and lip balm. Then I'm ready to clean, homeschool, cook, do laundry, and run a business, all while nursing the baby. Some days I may not get a chance to shower early in the morning. When that is the case, I make sure that I get one before my husband gets back, even if it's right before he walks in. There is more to what a man finds attractive than clothing. Overall, they want you to look inviting. That look will differ from man to man, but I can guarantee they all want their wives to look clean, neat, and refreshed.

The world tells women that they have to look a certain way so that their husbands won't look at other women. Men don't look at other women because their wives don't dress nicely. They do it because of the sin in their own hearts. A man's eye doesn't wander because his wife wore the wrong thing. If it were about the outfit, he would go and buy it for her to put on. Now, if your husband specifies a way in which he would like you to dress, then make it happen, but don't dress out of fear of losing him. When leaving the house together, dress in a way that will make him proud. Men see the way that their wives dress as a reflection of themselves. If their wife looks unkempt, it's a blow to their ego. A man wants his woman to stand out amongst others so he can proudly say, "that one is mine."

We should keep our bodies in good physical shape. For better or for worse is not a license to let yourself go. Loving you for who you are does not mean accepting excessive weight gain. Your weight is not who you are. If fitness is an area of struggle for you, then you should definitely pray for the motivation to improve your body through eating habits and exercise. Stay in shape so that you will be healthy, attractive, and so that you will be fit for sex.

If you can't maintain a position because your legs or arms are giving out, then you need to get workout. Do some squats. Lift some dumb bells. Don't deny your husband sexual satisfaction because you lack muscle. Don't miss out on your pleasure because you're easily tired.

Sex is for wives, too. When we climax, our bodies release chemicals that make us feel happier. These chemicals relieve stress and even pain. The more sex we have with our husbands, the more connected we are, and the better we feel.

Some struggle with sexual perversion: having an unhealthy view of sex. The source may be childhood sexual abuse, pornography, fornication, or infidelity. Jesus is Lord of your sex life too, and he wants to heal and give you a renewed mind. The world has perverted sexual intimacy and fraudulently tried to own it. Make no mistake about it. Sex came from the mind of God. He gave it to us to enjoy within the confines marriage.

The Soul

The soul's comprised of the heart and mind. It is the seat of the emotions and the source of thoughts. The soul processes knowledge and experiences in order to form a will, then it carries out that will through the body. When the bible refers to the flesh, it is actually referring the soul, for it is the soul that is corrupt. The body is just the medium by which the soul operates in the physical world.

When our souls become one, we bond on a more intimate level. We share secrets, dreams, and insecurities. This is the level at which most people have limited access. Our parents brought us into the world and raised us. However, even they don't know everything about us. In the parental relationship, the soul (mind and heart) is shaped, but not fully engaged. When we are growing up, we form opinions and world views based on knowledge, experience, and influences. We learn values and how to interact with others. We show different facets of ourselves to different people. Friends may see a side of you that parents never have. The marriage relationship is unique in that your spouse has the chance to see more of the soul than any other person.

Over the course of a marriage, you spend the most time with your spouse. The main reason why you have the chance to know your spouse in ways that others will not is because of the nature of the relationship. Marriage engages the soul in every area. Even a person's best attempt at hiding parts of themselves will fail in time, and their true self will be exposed. It's just like buying a used car. You can check the mileage, pop the hood, kick the tires, and even have your mechanic look at it. Only driving it over a period of time will expose any issues, but by then, it's yours. This sounds unfair and a little scary, but it is God's design.

Every human soul has been corrupted by sin. Our minds have been perverted on many levels. We are deeply broken. God wants to heal us of all of this brokenness and make it work for our good. He can use the institution of marriage to bring forth healing. Unfortunately, because of our self-centered attitudes, we miss opportunities to minister to our spouses. Even the unbeliever does this, so those who belong to Christ should be even better at it. We allow offenses to drive us away from each other instead of closer together.

There are reasons why God created marriage to last for a lifetime. One of which is that He foreknew that after the fall, we would be so profoundly broken that at the first sign of an issue, we would abandon each other. We have problems and insecurities that we will only share with someone who we know will not give up on us. "For better or for worse" means I will stick around for the fun and interesting parts of your soul, as well as the dark and ugly parts. As we recognize the darkness, we should bring healing to each other. This will be further discussed in the prayer section of this chapter.

On a lighter note, the Lord wants us to enjoy each other and explore uniqueness. We share information that we have learned, memories, humor, and dreams. We challenge each other's ways of thinking. It's natural for us to believe that our way is the right way. When we see that our husbands do things differently, we may think that he is wrong. Sometimes we are wrong, and when we realize it, the Lord uses the experience to keep us humble. This is how you grow in a marriage.

We should be gentle to the souls of our husbands so that we don't do too much additional damage. We should be loyal to our husbands by refraining from any actions or words that will betray his trust. Only give him full access to your soul and never verbally give anyone else full access to his soul. We must build the souls of our husbands by encouraging and respectfully challenging. Speak words of life into their soul. Finally, we must bring healing to their souls through prayer, tenderness, and long-suffering.

The Spirit

What is the spirit? Often times, spirit is used interchangeably with soul. This is true even in the bible, but they are not the same. The spirit is the innermost part of you. It is your identity. It is who God created you to be. God created Adam from the dust and then, the scripture says, he breathed into his nostrils and he became a living soul. The Hebrew translation for spirit is "ruach," which means breath. Without the breath (the spirit of God), the soul and body are dead.

God told Adam that in the day that he ate from the forbidden tree, that he would die. As soon as Adam disobeyed, he broke fellowship with the Lord. The spirit of the Lord left him. Death was immediate, but the manifestation was slow. Just like when a flower is plucked from a plant, it dies immediately. Even though it looks the same, eventually it will wither away. When Adam died spiritually, he was left with only his soul and body. That is, his mind and heart, and his body. Before, when Adam had the spirit of God in him, his heart and mind were governed by the Lord. He had access to unlimited knowledge and wisdom. His body executed what his soul processed from the Holy Spirit.

When the Spirit was no longer with him, his soul processed only what it perceived from the outside world. The flow was reversed. Since Adam and Eve no longer had fellowship with the Father, they had to make it in the earth the best they could with an enemy that was constantly plotting against them. Without the Spirit of God, they were no match for Satan and his demons. Before, Adam was influenced by the Spirit and his desire was that God would be glorified. Now, both he and Eve were influenced by Satan and their desire was that they would please themselves.

There is an age-old problem of men and women not understanding each other. There is even a book called "Men are from Mars, Women are from Venus." We seem to oppose each other in every area. God did make us very different, but his design was that we complement one another. The confusion is a result of sin. Before the fall, Adam and Eve were in sync with each other. Once they cleaved unto one another, they became connected even on a chemical level. I imagine that they stayed up late sharing thoughts and ideas and not arguing. I'm sure that after Adam brought down the entire creation, he didn't just carry on happily. He must have been sorrowful, confused, and angry. He was probably upset with Eve for bringing him the fruit.

When The Lord confronted Adam about what he had done, he basically blamed God and his wife. In Genesis 3:12, Adam explained, "The woman whom thou gavest to be with me, she gave me of the tree, and I did eat." Adam and Eve probably experienced guilt and resentment in their marriage; regret and fear. Now that they no longer had the presence of God, their marriage was wide open to the attacks of the Satan. The enemy probably began instigating and manipulating them to get them to separate. He tried his best to stop them from being fruitful and multiplying, as God commanded. He wanted to cut off the seed that would produce the redeemer who would crush his head.

God has already fulfilled his promise of a redeemer. He gave His son as a blood sacrifice to atone for the sins of man. Man can now have fellowship with God. God has also fulfilled His promise of sending the Holy Spirit. Man can now have the Holy Spirit live inside of him.

When a person is born again, their spirit comes alive again; yet, the soul is still sinful. "The heart is deceitful above all things and desperately wicked (Jeremiah 17:9)." In Romans 12:2, Paul writes, "And be not conformed to this world, but be ye transformed by the renewing of your minds." This means, do not allow your heart and mind to be shaped by the world, but constantly renew your mind through the word of God. With that being said, let's drive the point home.

In order to totally become one, both husband and wife must be spiritually alive. They must have the breath of God in them. They must be born again. Our identities and our purposes are in the Lord. In order to fully operate in our purpose, we must draw from Him. When the Spirit is in us, the mind thinks about the things of God. The heart desires what God desires.

> So, the deepest level of intimacy possible on earth is for one man and one woman to join together in matrimonial fellowship with God and minister

Then the body carries out the will of God. So, the deepest

level of intimacy possible on earth is for one man and one woman to join together in matrimonial fellowship with God and minister unto Him.

When we know what God's original design and intention was, we understand how the enemy manipulates us. Then we can strive for oneness. When we strive to become one, much of the confusion that couples experience will cease. When we are one, there is no room for the enemy to turn us against each other. We become more compassionate, we quickly forgive, and we remain focused because we know there is a greater goal ahead.

Oneness in the body means regular, uninhibited sex and intimate touching. Oneness in the soul means constant sharing of thoughts, ideas, secrets, interests, feelings, and memories. Oneness in the spirit means submission to God as a unit, seeking God as a unit, and finally carrying out His will for your specific marriage through the bodies.

When both the husband and the wife are born again, they have the potential to bond on all levels. It will take a lot of work and yielding to the Holy Spirit, but it is possible to experience all that God intended. If one spouse is a believer and not the other, then they can still be one in soul and body. The believing spouse can cover the unbeliever in prayer and intercede for them, believing that their spirit will be quickened. If neither spouse is born again, then they can still bond in soul and body.

Service

Serve in the right areas

In order to serve well, we must first understand what our God-given roles are. As outlined in the beginning of the book, the wife is the help meet. That is very general, so each wife must understand how to be the best help meet to her husband. The best way to know this is to ask your husband and to pay attention to him.

You do not want to work diligently in an area that your husband does not care much about, while neglecting the areas where he needs you the most. Your husband will be constantly unsatisfied because his needs are not being met and you will feel unappreciated. Although you are actively serving, you are serving in the wrong areas. This can become an ongoing conflict that can be deeply hurtful to both of you.

Since I love to cook so much, I tend to spend a lot of time in the kitchen. I also make many different types of meals, some of which take a lot of time to prepare. Dinner is not as big a deal to my husband as a clean house is. So, I can't spend a lot of time cooking an elaborate meal and then get defensive when he says the house is not clean. Once I truly understood the concept of serving in the right areas, I changed up my routine.

Anyone with kids knows that cleaning up is an endless job, and a clean house only lasts for 20 minutes or so. The children and I normally began the day with cleaning and did it again in the afternoon. However, by the time Kardell returned home, I was finishing up dinner, the house was a mess, and the kids were running around. He would immediately get frustrated when he walked in and saw things out of order. I would get defensive and run down all the things that I had to do that day. In my mind, he was not giving me credit for the many things that I did daily. From his perspective, he was leaving the stressful workplace and coming home to the thing he hates the most: a messy house. So, one day I decided we would spend the entire day deep cleaning. I made sure to use carpet powder and air freshener, too (he really likes the smell of cleaners and fragrances). When he came home, he was happy and impressed. Then he asked, "What's for dinner?"; to which I replied, "Nothing." I couldn't wait for him to ask so that I could show him that I couldn't do it all. He didn't care, though. It actually backfired on me because it showed me that I was slaving in the area that I loved to serve in and not the area that was most important to him.

Now, of course he doesn't always have to choose between dinner and a clean house. I did find ways to balance everything. I started having the kids clean the house before bed to eliminate the morning chores. I then made the second cleaning close to the time of his return so that he could actually see it while it was clean. At times when I don't have much time to clean, I just make sure to at least clean what he will see when he first walks in, and the area where he will rest in. Some days he will come in and the place will just be a disaster. That's okay. Everyone misses the mark sometimes, but the goal is to strive to serve diligently: first to please God and secondly to please our mates. When your heart is in the right place and you excel on a regular basis, then when you make a mistake or need a break, there is no shame or guilt.

You must first seek to please God because He is the author of marriage and because He is unchanging. Our husbands, on the other hand, will do things that make us not want to serve wholeheartedly or at all. Sometimes you will have to do it for God only. Be obedient to the glory of God. Wash his clothes to the glory of God. Have sex when you don't want it to the glory of God. That mindset will help you get through when you feel hurt, angry, or just slothful.

Another reason you must seek to please God first is because our service does not guarantee that our husbands will do right. Yes, good service can inspire them to be good to us, but we can do everything right and they still may choose to sin against us I mean, Jesus is the perfect husband and His bride sins against him continually.

The world tells us that a clean house, a hot meal, and regular sex will "keep" our husbands. Men have been made out to be sub-humans who only have physiological needs; as long as those needs are met, he will not stray. That is not true. Men stray for various reasons, many of which have nothing to do with what their wives are or are not doing at home. Of course we should do our very best because we do not want to leave room for the enemy to tem.pt them, but our service must be unto God because it may not be appreciated or reciprocated. No matter what happens in our marriages, we will stand alone on judgement day and answer for how we lived our lives. God's judgement will not be relative to how our husbands treated us, but rather directly based on His word.

Diligence

Whatever we do should be done well and done wholeheartedly. We should strive for excellence. When serving in marriage, we are being watched by many; but most importantly, by God. We should not settle for mediocrity in any area, but seek to improve in all areas. The Lord will show you when it's time to come up higher in a particular area. Think of the area that you struggle in the most with serving your husband and determine if you are doing enough or anything at all to improve. Reading this book is another step in the right direction. You may want to find more books on the subject or find someone who is willing to teach you and hold you accountable. Most importantly, ask God for wisdom. James 1:5 says, "If any of you lack wisdom, let him ask. God that

> When serving in marriage, we are being watched by many; but most importantly, by God. We should not settle for mediocrity in any area, but seek to improve in all

giveth to all men liberally, and upbraideth not and it shall be given him." Upbraid means to scold. The Lord holds all wisdom, knowledge, and resources. Surely, He will give you all that you need to do what He has called you to do.

As outlined in Proverbs 31, the virtuous woman was not one who stopped as soon as she got tired. She continued on into the late hours. She was determined to accomplish the work for her household. She was truly diligent.

Diligence is the resolve to consistently produce excellence. We should be more diligent in serving our husbands than serving any other human being. That means you must serve your husband with more diligence than you do your boss, pastor, or father. They have to get in line behind your man. We also have to continue working diligently even when we are upset with our husbands. What if we only served as long as we thought they deserved it? What if the Lord was only as generous to us as we were righteous?

When Kardell and I first married, we were barely adults and very immature. I was always very willing to serve and I actually enjoyed it, but there was a clause to my service contract. If he offended me, I shut it all down. "I mean why should I wash your clothes if you raised your voice at me?" was the way that I thought. One particular time, I was mad at him for something he did. Instead of snapping back, I said in my mind, "You will be surprised when you wake up and discover you have no lunch for work." I stiffly laid down next to him that night feeling victorious. Guess who interrupts my sleep? The Holy Spirit.

He plainly said, "Make his lunch." I thought to myself, "I don't know if that was the Lord. Maybe it was just me (as if I would go against what I wanted to do). If I hear it again, I'll know it's Him." Again, the Holy Spirit said, "Get up and make his lunch." I didn't want to do it, but I was too afraid to disobey, so I got out of bed and went to make Kardell's lunch. That night, the Lord taught me that I had to serve no matter what. As I separated my service from my emotions, it became easier for me to serve in sadness, anger, and disappointment. Now, I can be red hot and still fix a picture perfect plate. In fact, I serve so gracefully that a few times when he knew that I was mad, he jokingly cut his eyes toward me and asked if I poisoned the food. The loving kindness of God will confound people.

Initiative

A good servant does not have to be called upon very much. A good servant observes, anticipates, and executes before a word is spoken. You come into the marriage with an understanding of some of the things a wife should do. These things you should do to the best of your ability immediately. Other things you will learn to do as you get to know your husband. You will learn his needs, desires, and preferences. Once you know something, you become responsible for it. You cannot allow emotions or slothfulness to hinder you from serving in your full capacity. Remember, you are serving the Lord first, so don't wait to be called upon.

If you find that your husband consistently asks you for a particular thing, seek to anticipate the request next time. If he frequently comes home from work famished, then you ought to have something already prepared. Even if you are unable to have dinner complete, have something on hand to hold him over. If he is always asking for more clean socks, figure out a laundry schedule that will ensure that he never runs out. I'm sure you have figured out how often he wants sex and the indicators that he's ready. Do you ignore them and wait for him to ask, or even hope that he doesn't ask?

For the most part, my husband does not have to ask me to do anything; although, in the past, I struggled in two areas with taking initiative. The first area is cooking breakfast, which I do not like to do. My husband loves breakfast foods. He likes the full sausage, eggs, toast, grits, and juice spread. The kids are satisfied with oatmeal and I am happy with a smoothie or cold pizza. Many times, I waited for his request for breakfast and even then, I was reluctant. Eventually I just decided to anticipate by having his food ready before he woke up or upon arriving home from a midnight shift. I actually began to enjoy serving him breakfast because I knew that he loved it.

The second area that I struggled with was sex. It wasn't that I did not want it, but it was because of the timing. I tend to be a busy body and a night owl. He goes to bed early. I want sex to be a treat at the end of the day, when my mind is clear. It's hard for me to be interested when I know I have to get back to something else. I also don't want to still hear kids turning in their beds and asking for water. I need them all in REM sleep before I'm ready. My husband cares not. Kids can be knocking on the door and it won't bother him.

There were times when I knew that he was waiting for me and I would try to finish everything around the house, change into pajamas, brush my teeth, and put on moisturizer; and by the time I was ready, he had fallen asleep. There really was no room for compromising on this one because I knew he had to get up for work very early. I couldn't ask him stay up. I must admit, many times when I saw that he was asleep, instead of waking him up, I would start on something else. What I should have done was arrange my day to anticipate his needs and meet them without him saying a word.

When you have to continually ask someone to do something for you, it puts you in a position that makes you feel like you are begging. It seems that the person does not want to do anything for you and you can't help but to feel like a burden. This is not how your husband should be made to feel. If your heart is in the right place but you are just overwhelmed, you should ask for help. Ask the Lord for wisdom, ask other wives for advice, or ask your husband for help. Sometimes you need him to lift a burden off of you so you can serve him better. Do not expect him to read your mind. You can ask him to help you around the house so that you will be more available to him when he needs you.

Marriage is a ministry. Ministry just means service. We cannot expect to have marriages that thrive if we are not willing to serve. God is watching and our acts are being recorded for judgement day. The world is watching because they are looking for an answer and a hope for their own issues. Serve to the glory of God. Serve to the satisfaction of your husband.

Pray

If you ask any Christian couple what the key to marriage is, more than likely they will tell you prayer. Prayer is almost a cliché answer. Cliché in that, people say it without necessarily understanding how or why? Prayer is the key to marriage but the prayers must be specific and based on God's word.

Our prayers must be defensive and offensive. They must be proactive and reactive. Defensive and offensive implies that the fight is against an entity, which it is. Demonic forces constantly wage war on our unions. Ephesians 6:2 tells us that "we wrestle not against flesh and blood but against principalities, against powers, against the rulers of the darkness of this world, against spiritual wickedness in high places." Proactive and reactive is in reference to all other events and circumstances, whether natural or physical.

Praying for your husband is critical. Men are the heads of the household by title, even if they are not in position. They carry a very heavy burden. When someone is carrying something that is very large, heavy, and valuable, they need someone to watch for them. Imagine someone bringing a very large and expensive item into the house. They don't need help carrying it, but it's so big that they can't see everything clearly. They need you to spot them. So, you check out the surroundings. You warn them when there is a tight squeeze. You clear out trip hazards on the floor that may cause them to fall and drop the loads. You may have to tell them to slow down, shift left, or shift right.

A woman should do the same for her husband. It is her job to pray for him continually. Often times, a wife has insight in an area that her husband does not yet see. Her job is to pray for him in that area and respectfully warn him. A woman cannot force her husband to do anything. Forcing him may mean doing something in disobedience, controlling through emotional manipulation, or withholding service. If he does not take heed, then she must put it in God's hands because if she goes any further, she will be out of order.

I frequently remind my kids of the difference between power and authority. Power is simply the ability to take action. Authority is the permission to take action that has been delegated from a higher rank.

Right now, my second oldest, Zoey, has been stepping up to her role as big sister. I teach her that, as a big sister, if she sees a younger child doing something that they should not be doing, she should not turn a blind eye. One day, her younger brother, Kardell Jr., decided that he wanted to put his plate on the table without a placemat. Zoey rightfully told him to use a placemat. He refused. She continued to repeat herself and he continued to resist, so the situation intensified. Next, they were in a physical tussle and screaming match as she tried to shove a placemat under his plate while he tried to stop her. When I intervened, I addressed Zoey first. She was nearly in tears explaining that she was trying to get him to follow the rule that I made. Zoey was right in that she was trying to walk in her role as big sister and trying to correct the wrong. However, when she saw that he would not hear her, she should have brought the issue to me.

At the point where she got physical with him, she was using power without authority; so she had gotten herself into trouble right along with her brother. I told her that she was in the wrong. In her mind, she didn't understand why I was not fussing at Kardell Jr. first. If I had addressed him first, then she would have interpreted that as me backing up her actions. Even if I got on her case next, she still would have walked away feeling justified.

This is often the case in marriage. As wives, we try to correct our husbands according to what's right, and if they don't hear us, we repeat ourselves. Then we come from another angle. If that doesn't work, we try to manipulate through anger or sadness. If that doesn't work, we decide we will deny sex, conversation, dinner, or whatever we feel will be a sufficient punishment. If we try to force our spouse to take heed to what we say, we are using power without authority, and therefore are interfering with God's correction.

If a husband is doing something that is truly wrong and we try to straighten them out ourselves, then we will delay God's correction. Why? Because God is a God of order, and when He moves, everything must be in its proper place. He will continue to correct you and it will appear that the other person is getting away with it. So, if you have been praying that the Lord move on your husband's heart, yet you are still trying to evoke change on your own, then you are interfering with the very thing that you are praying for.

Prayer Cues

As mentioned in the section about the soul, no one will ever know a man like his wife. A man only shows a part of himself to other people, but his wife sees it all, whether he wants her to or not. Not even his mother will know him as intimately. A wife needs only to pay attention. That is how she will know how to pray for her husband.

In order to pray effectively for your husband, you must have a God-centered approach, as opposed to a self-centered approach. A self-centered approach says, "be a better husband to me." A God-centered approach says, "be made whole by God." Everything that a man does and does not do is reflective of his relationship with the Lord in that particular area of his life. When we have the right mindset, then our prayers are more effective in that they address the root brokenness in the man, and not just the fruit of the brokenness.

Praying for the fruit of the brokenness may sound like, "Lord please give my husband a heart to help around the house" or "Dear God, stop him from making foolish decisions." Those sound like sincere prayers but to be frank, those prayers are shallow and will only provide a temporary relief. If you want your husband to help around the house more, then you should identify the root of the problem and pray for that. If he is just lazy, pray that the Lord make him a diligent worker. If he doesn't seem to care how overwhelmed you are, pray that God gives him a heart of compassion. A man who makes foolish decisions may be operating hastily out of fear, or he may just be selfish and short-sighted. Don't just pick off the fruit. Find the root.

Everyone knows that running a lawn mower over weeds will not get rid of them permanently. If you want to get rid of them permanently, you must destroy them at the root and then reoccupy the soil with grass. If you do not plant grass seeds where the weeds were, then the area will be open for other seeds to land and take root.

Sometimes we can have the same issues in our marriages over and over again but in a different form. If we are not looking at the big picture, it can seem like we have never-ending issues that are all over the place; when in reality, all of the issues are manifesting from the same root, but in different areas of our lives. I will try to wrap up all of these ideas with an example from my own marriage.

Many times, I have gotten angry at my husband for not doing something in a timely manner. When we are getting ready to go somewhere, he waits until the last minute to get dressed. If we are preparing for a big dinner and I ask him to clean the house, when everyone arrives, the floor will be drying from being freshly mopped. I am a planner and I don't like to take chances, so his last-minute behaviors make my blood boil. I would get angry about it all the time.

Another thing that irritated me was his disorderliness. He has left his keys in the door all night several times. He would lose his wallet on a weekly basis. One time, as we were leaving, he was carrying the baby carrier in one hand and a garbage bag in the other, and he almost threw my baby in the dumpster. True story. So you can understand why, in my mind, I'm saying "Get it together!"

Early on in marriage our, I was just mad all the time. We argued because he took my keys to work because he couldn't find his own, then I couldn't leave the house. We argued because he waited until the last minute to resolve a business matter and the problem became worse. We argued because I texted him a grocery list that said two packages of small flour tortillas, but he came back with two small packages of flour and some tortilla chips. True story. I was so focused on how his actions affected me that I was missing the cues.

The Lord gave me wisdom to zoom out a little. I noticed that he was most disorganized when he was very busy. He gets sleepless, junky, and irritable. I also noticed that, often times, when he was in a jam, it was not because he had so much to do, but because he waited until the last minute to do one task and it caused a ripple effect.

The disorderliness was a result of procrastination. He puts things off, then it piles up. The Holy Spirit took me even deeper. He procrastinates because he is overwhelmed. My husband even told me that sometimes he has so many things to do that he just does nothing. He gets overwhelmed because of fear. Whenever it is time for you to do something, fear emphasizes how long it will take, how difficult it will be, how many things could go wrong, and how you may fail anyhow. God has not given us a spirit of fear but a spirit of love, power, and a sound mind.

With this revelation, I first had compassion on him. I realized that it wasn't that he just didn't care about how his actions affected me; it was that he was broken in an area and needed healing. Now, of course he is able to make some adjustments to the way that he operates. I mean, when he tries really hard, he can be more organized and timely. However, his efforts are behavior modifications, which can only last for so long. All the while, the inner turmoil is still going on. The right conditions will bring that flaw right back out, just like a weed. So, once the weed is removed, then grass needs to be planted.

In my husband's case, that grass would be the peace of God. Once he allows the peace of God into that broken area of his life, then no matter how great the burden is or how numerous the responsibilities are, he won't be captured by fear. He will be able to navigate life with the peace of God and the manifestations will be organization, timeliness, and thoroughness.

I also had to realize that I am the helper. I had to stop viewing his shortcomings as something that he needed to fix, and start viewing them as an opportunity to help. With this understanding, I started anticipating his needs. I made hooks for the keys so that he wouldn't misplace them as much. I reserved a drawer for his wallet and any other important things that he may have needed to take with him. I started sending him reminder texts for bills and other matters. Thus, I switched from telling him that he needed to be more organized, to becoming his personal organizer.

Defensive prayer

Ephesians 6:18 says, "Praying always with all prayer and supplication in the spirit and watching thereunto with all perseverance and supplication for all saints." This scripture, like many others, tells us to watch. In order to know what to pray for, we must be watchful of the attacks of the enemy. Safe and general prayers like, "Dear Jesus, bless our marriage" won't fortify your marriage. Ephesians 6:12 says that we wrestle against principalities, powers, and the rulers of the darkness of this world. Therefore, our prayers must be specific and targeted at those forces.

You may recognize that your husband is struggling with something dark. It may not even be that obvious. Maybe you just sense something is off with him. Begin to pray against the powers that influence him in that area. Pray with him. Pray for him and lay hands on him in his sleep. Rebuke the enemy's work in his life. Resist the temptation to fight against him regarding the matter because it really won't be productive. Even if he does modify his behavior, the roots will only breakthrough in another area of his life, and you will be dealing with the same problem in a different form. Trying to solve the problem in your husband will only damage him further.

Let God work

If a person has been shot, it is critical that they get to a hospital to be treated professionally. The person who helps the victim should only do what is absolutely necessary to keep the person alive, while getting them to the emergency room as quickly as possible. Once at the hospital, x-rays will reveal the path of the bullet and vitals will determine

One Flesh

the overall condition of the person. Before the surgeon begins the extraction, they already have a plan and they know what could potentially go wrong. Sometimes they may postpone extraction until a time where the patient is more stable.

What if, instead of taking the victim to the hospital, the helper decided they would extract the bullet? Assuming that this person has no training, that would be a terrible idea. Imagine if they tried to dig the bullet out with their fingers. If they go in blind trying to find the bullet, they could destroy other organs in the process. Even if they can see exactly where the bullet is, removing it may cause hemorrhaging. Don't forget that they're lacking anesthesia, so more pain will be inflicted onto the victim. If the bullet was successfully removed without incident, the risk is not over. The wound could become infected later. Also, it needs to be properly closed up. So, needless to say, the best option is to just apply pressure to the wound and get the person to the hospital.

Every human being has been shot. Some have superficial wounds and some very deep ones. Some bullets have been lodged in areas that are not so life-threatening, and some have ripped through many layers and destroyed organs. Husbands have been shot; and our job, as wives, is to get them to the Surgeon, who is Jesus.

Trying to perform the surgery on our own can be disastrous for our husbands and our marriages. The Lord knows exactly where they are hurt and broken. He knows when they are ready for extraction. He will administer anesthesia to numb the pain. He will gently peel back the layers of their lives and be sure not to damage them emotionally, mentally, or physically. His scalpel is sharper than any two-edged sword, and His hand is steady and accurate. When He gets the bullet out, He won't leave anything behind before He closes the wound. Unlike our tools, His tools are sterile. Our tools of punishment, manipulation, persuasion, and reasoning are contaminated and can infect the patient with sadness, defeat, anger, and resentment. So, the best thing we can do is apply pressure to the wound, in the form of love and compassion, and pray in the waiting room while the Great Physician operates.

Offensive Prayer

Do not limit your prayers to what you think your husband is capable of doing or not doing. Only the Lord knows what we are fully capable of. "The heart is deceitful above all things and desperately wicked. Who can know it (Jeremiah 17:9)?" He may even surprise himself. So, you do not have to wait on the enemy to attack an area for you to pray against it. Sometimes you have to go into the enemy's camp when they least expect it.

If you know of or recognize a particular issue that your husband's family has dealt with continually, that is a good area to start. There may be issues of sickness, addiction, violence, adultery, divorce, sexual perversion, lawlessness that leads to imprisonment, or depression, to name a few. If you see there is a pattern, then cover your husband in prayer in that area.

It doesn't matter if your husband is "different" from the men in his family. Cover him. It is not the identity of men that causes them to struggle in these areas; it is the forces of darkness that influence them and seek to devour them. So you can be sure that the enemy wants your husband, who is "different," even more so, especially if he is a believer.

Neither you nor your husband know what seeds the enemy has planted in his life that can grow into destructive behaviors that will choke out his life and the life of your family. In the winter time, most things are in a resting state. Grass is brown, trees have no leaves, there are no flowers, and no bugs are out. However, those things are not dead. They are in a resting state, awaiting the right conditions for them to flourish again. The right temperature and sunlight will cause growth. The same is true for the seeds that husbands carry in their hearts and minds. The right conditions in his life can cause those things to grow. Maybe he can handle serious financial issues with grace. However, financial issues combined with a new baby on the way may be the right conditions for that seed of depression to grow. Ask the Holy Spirit to give you a battle plan specifically for your man.

> **Our goal in praying for our husbands should not be to have a better husband nor a better marriage. The goal should be to intercede in order that they be healed, made whole, set free**

Our goal, in praying for our husbands, should not be to have a better husband nor a better marriage. The goal should be to intercede in order that they be healed, made whole, set free, and love God. A better husband and marriage will follow. When the resurrection power of Christ is manifested in their lives, they will be better in every area of their lives, including marriage. To truly love our husbands is to remove ourselves from the prayer and genuinely pray on their behalves. When our prayers are pure, we cause God to move according to His will. To be clear I will give a few examples.

Let's say your husband does not work hard or at all. If you pray "God make him work," your husband may have a season of working and then go back to being slothful. However, if you pray, "Lord heal the brokenness in him that prevents him from providing," you watch the hand of God move. Things will begin to happen and it will probably hurt a lot, but He will accomplish the work.

Understand that the areas in your husband's life that need to be healed may never be recognized by another human being. I mean, some levels of brokenness are so deep that it takes decades to finally identify. You may be the only person who ever looks beyond the behavior on the surface, and as a wife, you hold a level of authority that no one else holds. This is the sacredness of marriage. Despite our own brokenness, we carry in us the potential to bring healing to our husbands through Christ. We must see through the eyes of Christ!

Aspiring Wives

If you are a single woman looking for a husband, stop. Nowhere in scripture will you read about a woman searching for a man. It is always the man finding the woman. You can either trust God to bring you to the husband that you desire, or you can try to find the right one on your own. You may still marry the one that God intended for you, but you may enter the marriage at the wrong time and go through unnecessary pain.

God does not have to figure out whom to send you. However, He does have to prepare both of you first. Make sure it is not you that is holding up the wedding. You may be waiting for a long time because your husband is praying for a woman who can throw down in the kitchen, and you still haven't learned how to cook. Love him before you meet him.

A woman should prepare for a husband. Submit yourself to Christ. Seek Him with all of your might. Take classes, get advice, read books, and watch videos. Prepare yourself to be a helper. Do not invest all of your time in your physical appearance. That will not attract your Boaz. I'm not saying that you should not be pleasing to the eyes, but do not believe the lie of the world that your body is what will draw him to you. Gain home skills in preparation for marriage. Get ahead of the game and learn how to pray for him, encourage him, and talk to him. If you are faithful to Jesus and prepare for what you say you believe, He will bless you with that man and he will be drawn to you even on an ugly day.

A single woman should look at a potential husband the way she would a potential job. Hopefully you won't accept a job just because they are hiring. Before you commit your time to one employer and turn down other opportunities, you want to be sure that you are making the best decision. You should look at the employer's past and examine their reputation. Do they treat employees right? Is there a high turnover rate? See how they interact with the current workers.

You definitely want to know how they handle business. Do they compensate fairly? Do they have integrity? Is the overall business in growth or decline? You wouldn't want to work for a company that is going out of business, especially if you have children to feed. You must know these things before you get onboard because once you submit to them, you will not have the authority to change the way that they run the business. You will not have the authority to tell the boss that their business practices are destructive. Even if you are right, they will likely reject what you say because you are a subordinate.

Once you marry a man, it is not your job to come in and change the direction in which his life is headed. It is your job to serve and support his vision. If he does not have a vision, no matter how hard you work or what you do to move you all ahead, it will not work. Not because your husband is holding you back, but because you will be in mutiny. God does not advance those who are in rebellion. So, before you agree to follow a man and support his vision, you need to know his reputation, inquire about his past relationships, and observe his interactions with his friends and family. Is he wise? Does he love God? Is his life headed in the right direction? If you already have children, will they benefit from the marriage? These are things you must know, because once you say "I do" ... you have to. You have to submit and you have to serve.

Before you agree to submit yourself to a man, find out where he is headed. Know what his definition of marriage is. Everyone has their own understanding of what marriage is based on teaching and experiences. We cannot assume that another person has the same interpretation.

Imagine marriage as getting on a bus. Have you ever gotten on the wrong bus? You hop on in a rush and pay your fare. At first, you are enjoying the ride until the driver makes that first wrong turn. You start looking confused. You think "maybe they are taking a detour." Then they make another turn. You grow more and more anxious as you realize they are not taking you where you want to go. Then you get up and walk to the front to ask the driver where he is going. In the exchange, you realize that you got on the wrong bus. You were expecting the driver to take you somewhere that he never said he would. He had the destination clearly flashing across the windshield, but you didn't look. Now you are somewhere that you did not intend or want to be, but you can't blame him. You ignored the sign and you never asked him. He was just driving. Ladies, before you get on the bus, read the sign, check the route, talk to the people at the bus stop, and ask the bus driver to verify his destination.

Chapter 5
Train Up a Child

Children are a heritage of the Lord and the fruit of the womb is His reward. Psalms 127:3. The scripture tells us that children are a blessing. We must treat them as such. Children are not hindrances of our hopes and dreams. If we feel that way, then we have the wrong view and we must allow the Lord to transform our minds in this area. As mothers, we must be dedicated to nurturing our children, not babysitting.

I have five children and my oldest is ten years old, but I still feel like I am fairly new at being a mother. The Lord has blessed me with His wisdom, but he has also given me to be a very observant person. I glean from the lives of others and apply the knowledge to my own life. In the process of writing on child-rearing, I began to feel like I did not have enough wisdom in this area to write about it. So, I did not write another sentence until I heard from the Lord; and heard from the Lord I did. He spoke to me that training a child is not so much about techniques as it is about working toward a goal. We must focus on a macro level and not a micro level.

The goal of raising children is to produce a person who is ready to serve God and bring him glory. Malachi 2:15 tells us that God seeks a Godly offspring. In order to produce godly offspring, we must cultivate their souls, make them feel loved, discover their purpose, give them life skills, teach them to fear God, and train them to continue the God-given order of the family. Techniques will vary from family to family and from child to child. The only requirement is that they be in line with scripture.

Cultivate

Often times, we get so overwhelmed with day-to-day struggles that we lose sight of the goal that is before us. We search for answers on how to get children to do this and how to get them to stop that. We must realize that their behavior is just a signal for us to cultivate their souls. Let's pause for a second and define cultivate: to prepare and work on in order to raise crops.

I am an amateur gardener. A couple years back, I had quite a few crops growing in my backyard: tomatoes, bell peppers, zucchini, carrots, lettuce, snow peas, you name it! I was so excited to eat food that I had actually grown from seed. If you know anything about gardening, then you know that it is a lot of work. From the time that you put the seed in the ground to the time of the harvest, there are threats at every stage. Birds will eat the seeds as soon as you sow them. You have to pull out the weeds that will suck up all of the water and nutrients and block the sun. You have to till the dirt to keep the soil loose and ensure that the tender roots are able to stretch out. The battle against root-eating insects is constant. You have to make sure that the plant stays rooted in the ground. When the plant is established and begins to bear fruit, then come the rodents that try to eat your crops! All this and you still have to water them and till the soil every day. Gardening was no joke, but the thought of eating a salad with lettuce and tomatoes from my own backyard was what kept me going. The Lord taught me that child-rearing is a lot like gardening.

From the moment of conception to the time that they become adults, there are threats at every stage. During pregnancy, there are so many issues that can arise that threaten the life of the child. Giving birth to a child is nothing short of a miracle. When they are born into the world, there are even greater challenges ahead. Their immune systems must be prepared to take on the sicknesses and diseases of the world. They have to be protected from people who mean them harm. They have to be defended from the attacks of Satan. They have to be shielded from the culture and the wisdom of the world. In addition to all of this, they still have to be fed, bathed, hugged, dropped off and picked up, and taught.

You can see the parallel between gardening and raising children. Every day I would go out into the yard to check on the plants. Wilted leaves indicated a need for water. If the edges of the leaves were brown, I knew they needed shade. Leaning toward the ground meant that they needed to be straightened up and maybe supported with a stake. When I saw bite marks on a tomato plant, I knew that I needed to put chicken fencing around it to keep out rodents.

We have to approach parenting in the same way. What we see in our children are indicators that we need to till the garden of their souls. Our focus cannot be to get our kids to "act right". Instead, we must train them so that they have a well of righteousness to draw from.

Some children throw tantrums when they can't have their way. Kicking and screaming indicates a need for self-control. Rebellion indicates a need for teaching on respect for authority. When our children behave badly, they are showing us the areas where they need God the most. This is the macro level. If we only respond with a consequence to try to get them to "act right," then we are focusing on the micro level. A child who is only trained to perform will only do so as long as they are aware of a potential immediate consequence. Proverbs 4:23 says, "keep thy heart with all diligence; for out of it are the issues of life." What is in the heart will eventually overflow. We must recognize undesirable behavior as cues to cultivate.

It can be frustrating to deal with the same issue with children over and over again. "How many times do I have to tell you?" Don't we know that it will be again and again? It would be silly to go out into a garden and say, "Huhhhh, the zucchini needs water again! Aww, man. The tomatoes, too?" We have to keep in mind that children will need to be watered with godly teaching daily; better yet, hourly. When plants are young, they have to be watered frequently because their tiny little roots can only draw up so much water. Too much water at once will drown them. When they become mature plants, they can go a couple days without water because their roots will grow deeper into the ground and further out. Small children need to be corrected by the minute. The older they get, the more they can retain, and correction will be less frequent.

When I started gardening, I understood that wilted plants need water and leaning plants need straightening. However, when I became more experienced, I learned to anticipate the needs of the plants rather than wait until they were in trouble. I would check the weather and prepare them to be able to fair well. If it would be a hot day, I would water them thoroughly at night. In Michigan, frost can come at any time. Some nights I had to cover them with plastic and bedsheets so they would not freeze. I tilled around the plants every day and raked out potential weeds. When I took this approach, the work was not as tedious.

If we anticipate the needs of our children, we won't get blindsided by certain issues and behaviors. If we are intentional about teaching them God's ways, then we will have something to draw from when the issues arise. For example, when my daughter was 8 years old, I had to begin to teach her about sex and purity. I followed the old-fashioned, "say nothing until you absolutely have to model." I do not recommend this. Well, I had to scramble for wisdom, a lesson, and courage to quickly present to her before the weeds of the world choked out her tiny root of innocence. It went well, praise God, but it would have been better had I began with an age appropriate biblical model when she was much younger, and built from there.

So, God is telling us that we need to approach children the way we would approach gardening. We should expect to work and anticipate the needs. Why, then, do we get so frustrated with them when they are just letting us know what their needs are? The answer is simple but hard to admit. We are selfish and self-righteous.

As fallen beings, it is in our nature to look out for self-first. We walk a path of self-gratification and we do not like any detours down "Help Someone Out Lane." We don't want to have our sleep broken. We don't want to break up another fight. We don't want to be touched. We don't want to engage. We don't want to look. We don't want to listen. We don't want to explain, and correct, and teach. We want to live in a world of uninterrupted TV shows, book chapters, and phone-calls, peace and quiet, saying things once, and enjoying a treat with no beggars. God will not allow that because He wants to do a work in us. It is often said that children don't come with manuals. It is not God's intention to make the journey easy for us. It is His intention to allow us to go down a path that will bring to the surface anything that is unlike Him.

While we rear our children, God is rearing us, too. What? You thought it was just about them? No way! He uses children as a mirror for our eyes. He uses them as an echo for our ears. He uses them to remind us that our righteousness is as filthy rags. Have you ever struggled with something in your child, only to realize months later that they were emulating you? Have you ever done such a good job instilling something in your child that they used it on you? Of course! This is God's intent.

I remember I was teaching my kids from Galatians 5:22-23 about the fruit of the spirit: love, joy, peace, long suffering, goodness, faith, meekness, temperance. Well, Zoey struggles with temperance. She was born with zero self-control. She would yell, scream, and fall out for anything, anywhere, anytime, and in front of anyone. Maybe she got this from me because I struggle with yelling at my kids.

One day, Zoey was throwing a fit and I said to her "Zoey, you need to have self-control." As my lips came to form "self-control" and I projected it from my mouth, the Holy Spirit curved the sound of the words right back into my ears and used me to say to myself "You need to have self-control." I paused. I was so humbled and looked on her with more compassion instead of having a fed-up attitude. See, self-righteousness.

Children need to feel loved

One of the best things that I ever learned about was how people perceive love differently. This concept came from a book written by Gary Chapman called *The Five Love Languages*. Everyone has a different perception of what love is. They receive love and love others based on their love language. First, my husband and I took the test. It was very helpful and eye opening. Then, we tested our children. When we learned their love languages, it made it easier to love them in the way that they needed. It also revealed that a lack of love in their own language was the reason behind some misbehaving. Now that we know what our children perceive as love, we can use that as a guide to spending time with them.

Life can be busy and crazy, and carving out time to spend with one child can be difficult. Even more difficult is when you take time with the child and they are still not satisfied. Perhaps they continue to misbehave. Sometimes the problem is that what you did was not interpreted as love. They can appear to be ungrateful when in their mind, you still have not loved them. This is true in marriage as well, which we will discuss later.

Our oldest child's love language is "quality time." She loves being with the whole family and having everyone on one accord. In order to love her in a way that she will understand, you have to spend quality time with her. What does that mean? She wants more than to just talk to you. She wants to share ideas and ask you questions. Your mind must be fully present. You have to give her eye contact and feedback. She desires a mental connection. So, we can take her on an outing by herself and buy her things, but if there is no connection, then she will not feel the love; and guess what? You've just wasted your time and money because her love tank will still be on "E." An empty love tank means behavioral issues.

Our second child's love language is "words of encouragement." She is very sensitive and easily discouraged, but if you tell her something positive, she will do something good every time. When we spend quality time with her, she doesn't say much. We may be riding to get ice cream and she will sit silently the whole ride. I'll try to make conversation, but it doesn't go anywhere because she doesn't really want that. I can just say "you did so well at swim. You can be on the swim team one day." She will simply smile, but that would set her on fire. Then, when we get home, she will start doing nice things for others because her love tank is on full. We have yet to discover the love languages of our younger three, so until then, we will just try to cover them all. After all, it's easy to love them when they are still little and cute.

Love is the key to a child's heart. I do not mean that in a vague and cliché way. If your children know that you love them, then they will respect you and share their heart with you. Love is not a feeling. Love is service. It is a decision. This decision is simply whether or not you will act in another person's best interest as commanded by Jesus. Every day, you must decide to act in your child's best interest. If they are disobedient, is it in their best interest that they receive a consequence, or that you ignore it? If they are continually acting out, is it in their best interest to give them a hug because they need affection, or just continue to punish them?

Not all children are easy to love. Some people are afraid to admit that their kids get on their nerves or that they have a hard time loving them. That is okay. What is pleasing to the Lord is that we choose to love them despite their foolishness and how we feel. Jesus commanded us to love one another. He never said we had to like anyone. Wonder why? We cannot control whether or not we like someone. Some people just rub us the wrong way. However, we can absolutely control our love for one another. To love someone may be difficult, but it is simple. You offer your body as a vessel for God to fill and pour out on others. The difficulty is sharing what He so freely gives to us. We love them by teaching, correcting, encouraging, forgiving, and praying for them.

It is important to forgive our children. I don't just mean forgive them for stealing a cookie. I mean forgive them for being difficult to love. Forgive them for rebelliousness, ungratefulness, disobedience, throwing tantrums, and saying or doing things that hurt you. These are some of the issues that can cause a parent to be angry with their child continually. I mean, it's the next morning and you still aren't ready to see their face. They are fresh and happy, saying, "morning mommy," and your lips are still tightened. Jesus said we must forgive 7 x 70. He must have had my kids in mind when he said that because they have just about exhausted that quota. Good thing he really meant never stop forgiving.

Discovering their purpose

Children need help discovering their purpose and encouragement to walk in it. We get many clues from them every day, but we must pay close attention. Observe patterns, listen, and watch. Little by little, their talents, passions, and ultimately, their purpose will be revealed. If you give them plenty of exposure, then you can get a better idea of how they connect with the world and what interests them. Expose them to art, music, sports, sciences, and nature. This does not have to be expensive. There are so many experiences out there that are free of charge or minimal cost. If you look for it, you will find it. If you pray for it, the Lord will answer. Surely he will provide the tools needed to cultivate what He put in us.

If we are too focused on accomplishing our own dreams, then we can easily overlook our children's calling. That does not mean that they will not make it to where God would have them to be; it just means that you will not have had the privilege of being the primary cultivator. If you don't put in the blood, sweat, and tears now, then when the victories are won, you will be just an onlooker in the crowd. If this is true for you, there is still hope in redemption. Jesus can resurrect you, as well as a broken relationship with your child. Just do your best from this point forward.

- Pay attention to their interests.
- Ask them questions regularly.

- ⸱ Introduce them to new things.
- ⸱ Pay attention to what gets them into the most trouble and think about how it could be a strength in their life.
- ⸱ Invest your time and money into their interests and talents.
- ⸱ If they express an interest, take them seriously. Follow up.

Teach Them to Fear God

"Children obey your parents in the Lord: For this is right. Honour thy father and mother which is the first commandment with promise, That it may be well with the and thou mayest live long on the earth (Ephesians 6:1-3)." God gave parents authority over children and this authority should be reflective of His nature. We should practice love and justice. This means extending to them grace and mercy, and also chastisement. This will put the fear of God in them.

The bible says in Hebrews 12:6, "For whom the Lord loveth He chasteneth, and scourageth every son whom He receiveth." They not only need to understand right from wrong, but also that there will always be a consequence for sin. Proverbs 13:24 says, "He that spareth his rod hateth his son: but he that loveth him chasteneth him betimes." This means that if you truly love your child, then you will correct them early on. This way, when they get older, their hearts will be soft toward authority. If we withhold correction from our children, then we are failing to love them. We may fail to correct out of laziness, guilt, or our own childhood experiences. Whichever the case, it is rooted in selfishness. Teach them, as little ones, that violating God's law is dangerous. "Foolishness is bound in the heart of a child; but the rod of correction shall drive it far from him (Proverbs 22:15)." Help them to identify their specific sin nature and teach them to keep it under subjection.

"For all have sinned and fallen short of the glory of God (Romans 3:23)." We were all born in sin and shaped in iniquity. Our sins, though equal, are all different. Each child is born with a specific sinful disposition. If a parent does not recognize this sin nature and call it out, then a child can struggle with it throughout adulthood, never knowing exactly what the issue is.

Children should be trained to deal with their most prominent sin aptness. Say, for example that a child knows, at the age of seven, that they struggle with rage. Now that this area of sinfulness has been exposed, with training, by adulthood they can have a good handle on it. They can be taught to ask God to help them in this area, confess sin regularly, and avoid situations that will feed the sin.

As you recognize your child's most prominent sinful nature, you can prepare them by choosing a scripture to fight against it. Every time your child bears fruit from that root of sin, you cut it down and re-occupy the soil with the word of God. Those scriptures will be engrained in their soul and will begin to bare godly fruit.

When we deal with sin in children, we have to consider the root first, that predisposition. You may have two children that struggle with disobedience, but for different reasons.

One child may bear fruit of disobedience that it is coming from a branch of rebellion. That branch of rebellion is coming from the root of pride. When they disobey, it may be a very calculated decision. They consider all of their options and possible consequences. Once the decision is made, they execute. Disobedience for the sake of opposing authority is rebellion. Rebellion against righteous authority is pride.

The other child may disobey because they are forgetful or do not pay attention. "I forgot" should not excuse a child from a consequence. They may be forgetful because they are unorganized and impulsive. This child may bear fruit of disobedience coming from a lack of self-control. In both cases, the issue was disobedience, but the root cause was different. Once the root is identified, you can determine a plan of action tailored to the soul of each child.

I encourage my children to continually confess their sins to the Lord. I tell them to call on the name of the Lord in times of struggle and to speak scriptures to themselves. The enemy will tempt them in areas of weakness and they need to be aware of him and how he works. Eventually they will learn to avoid his traps. They can learn how to be victorious as children so that they don't have to spend decades as adults being defeated in the same area.

When dealing with sin, I always ask the child why they did it. "I don't know" is unacceptable. Everyone knows exactly why they do the things that they do. We use "I don't know" as an excuse because we know that the real reason is too shameful to say out loud. That statement is like the fig leaves that Adam and Eve used to cover themselves. I tell my kids to verbally express the reason why they did something. I want the real, raw reason. Usually it's "because I wanted to." When they speak the reason from their mouths and allow themselves (and me) to hear it, then the sin is exposed. They are forced to face just how ugly it is. This allows them to practice being honest with themselves and be naked before God. The enemy condemns us and wants us to keep our sin a secret so that he can water it to make it grow. We have to continually rake out those weeds so that we can allow our children to grow enough to defend themselves.

It is important to discuss your own sin nature with your children. They have to understand that we, too, are fallen beings that are subject to the word of God. When they understand that we struggle everyday as well, they will be more comfortable sharing their own struggles. When we give the impression that sin is not an issue for us, then they can be consumed by shame, guilt, and condemnation. They need to have a balanced understanding of what God thinks about sin. God hates sin but He is a merciful God. Also, He understands how we feel. The scripture says in Hebrew 4:15, "For we have not an high priest which cannot be touched with the feelings of our infirmities; but was in all points tempted like as we are, yet without sin." This scripture helps us understand that God is a God of compassion. He knows the struggles of the flesh and He wants us to set our brokenness before Him, and allow Him to fill the void.

> It is important to discuss your own sin nature with your children. They have to understand that we, too, are fallen beings that are subject to the word of God.

God's Order

As parents, our job is to prepare our children to continue God's order for the family. In order to do this, we must first know what that is for ourselves. Then, we must put it into practice to the best of our ability. If you are a single, separated, or widowed woman, you can do this. If you are a believer married to an un-believer, you can do it as well. The scripture says, "I can do all things through Christ which strengtheneth me (Philippians 4:13)."

Children need to know exactly what God intended for marriage, even if it will shine light on your past or current sins. They need to be taught extensively on the biblical purposes and boundaries of sex. If you shy away from this because you do not want to incriminate yourself, then you know what to do. You must abandon any relationship that is not Christ-centered. You are being watched and every action is a seed sown into the soul of your children. Any voids should be filled with Christ. No husband in the household? Let Jesus be your husband. Obey Him. Serve Him. Have intimacy with Him. Following this order will prepare both you and your children to receive your future husband, who will be the leader of the household.

Life Skills

When your children leave the household, they should be prepared to operate in their roles. They should not be thrust into life without a clue. Training begins early. I believe that when a child can walk steady, they should have some form of responsibility. This may come in the form of potty-training or even just "bring mommy the wipes." Early on, they need to understand that something is expected of them. It's not boot camp. They will be delighted to help. You will give them a sense of purpose and accomplishment. As the child matures, their responsibilities will increase. Every child and every household is different, but one thing is for sure: every child ought to be in training.

By nature, I am a do-it-yourself kind of person. I frequently said things to myself like "If you want it done right, do it yourself." I struggle with delegating tasks to anyone because I don't want to take the time to explain and correct. My kids used to ask to help me with household tasks and I would say "next time" because I was always in a rush. The Lord began to work this out of me when I was pregnant with my third child.

It was the most difficult pregnancy. I was sick at all times for the first four months; then when that was over, I had pain. I carried the baby on the left side of my belly, so there was a tremendous amount of pressure in my pelvis. So much so, that I felt like I could push him out if I tried. This triggered sciatic nerve pain. The sciatic nerve runs from the lower back to the feet. If you make the wrong move, the nerve becomes constricted and the pain will take you to the floor. If I sat too long, it would hurt to get up; I would need help. It took me minutes to lie down for bed. Some days when I would wake up, I had to mentally prepare to step out of the bed; and often times, I would collapse to the floor. I have had to crawl to the kitchen before. Sometimes I needed to sit in the driveway for 5 minutes to prepare to step out of the van. Other times I couldn't finish making dinner because the pain was too great. I could not keep up with the laundry because most days, I could not get down the steps. You get the point. It was hard. I became overwhelmed with housework and here I was about to have another baby.

One day I was washing dishes and crying out to the Lord. Lump in my throat, hot tears dropping, angry, had a little bit of that crazy laugh. I mean I was on the edge. I said "Lord, how am I supposed to do all of these things and I can barely walk? *You* want me to have children. Lord, show me what to do." Immediately he directed my attention to my two girls ages three and six who were sitting in the living room enjoying TV. I thought to myself "ya'll gone do this!" From that point forward, I began to give them more responsibilities outside of cleaning their room.

My oldest had been begging for this for so long. I taught her how to do laundry. I made her a chart of laundry categories based on color and fabric. I gave her permission to use the microwave, started teaching her to wash dishes, trained her to use a knife, and taught her how to make toast. I taught my three-year-old how to vacuum. Yes! She could handle that thing well, too. Oddly enough, she had already had a slight obsession with vacuum cleaners, so that was right up her alley. So, I began to train my girls to help around the house. I had to take some time out and they made some mistakes, but it took some pressure off of me and gave them a greater sense of responsibility. The Lord taught me something valuable through this experience.

More children does not have to mean a more difficult life. That is a lie of the enemy. God is not the author of confusion. If you develop a system, more children will actually mean a promotion for the existing family members. Obviously there will be a substantial initial investment. You will be tired and worn out with little ones who can't do much. Sleepless nights, diaper changing, chasing, and cleaning. If you train your children to share in family responsibilities as they become capable, your work should shift from labor-intensive to managerial.

It is difficult to clean up after one toddler and even more so after two. At some point, the oldest must "move out of the way." So as you have more children, you should not be performing the same tasks for each and every one. It should be a constant rotation so that no one remains in the same stage too long. If you are expecting a new family member, you need to train the existing family members for their new positions so that their current positions can be available. The system works itself.

Although the system works differently if you have a family member who cannot advance to the next stage, such as a special needs child, human beings are not burdens. A child who needs 24-hour care is just as valuable as the child who is independent and must be treated as such. We are all broken, inside and out. If you have a special needs child, then any other children in the house need to understand that they are supposed to share in the caretaking.

Birth maladies are a result of the sin of mankind. However, God foreknew just who would be born into the family, so the challenges that other members face in helping out can actually benefit them in their life journey. Yes, the child is ultimately the parents' responsibility, but each family member must contribute to the one who needs the most. Parents should not feel guilty about asking children for help, as if their lives are being infringed upon. Ironically, having such an attitude can teach the children just that. No, they did not ask for such a sibling, but neither did they ask to be born themselves.

Instill in them good character traits such as selflessness, responsibility, initiative, and endurance, then ask them boldly with the expectation that they will respond with a good attitude. If they respond with reluctance or an ugly attitude, show them what God's word says about love and kindness, then ask them again. And again…and…again…until their heart softens, because it is not about being "burdened" with a person who cannot do for themselves; it's just that the Lord used that situation to reveal the content of their heart. You can use this inside information to war for their soul. That is grace.

Chapter 6

Burn Out

If you strive to be a godly household manager, eventually you will come up against some heavy opposition. Whether it be natural or spiritual, specific or circumstantial, at some point you will feel discouraged, depressed, anxious, unhappy, or insecure. I speak as one with experience.

In the past two years or so, I began to feel emotionally unstable. I was easily overwhelmed and would cry over things that I normally would not. When it began, I was pregnant so it seemed normal. After I delivered the baby, I still had the same feelings, but it still seemed normal because of my circumstances. My family was in the middle of a major transition: we added a sixth family member and we had just moved a few weeks before the baby was born. To add another change, my husband switched to the night shift. As the months went on, I never adjusted. As a matter of fact, I began to feel worse. I went from anxious and overwhelmed to frustrated and angry. I felt like my once orderly life was now a spiraling mess.

We used to have a daily routine that worked. My husband and I went on dates regularly. I was free to leave and have time to myself even if it was just going to the grocery store after bedtime. Well, all of that changed because of our circumstances. I started looking back on "the good times." You know the period of time when things seemed great? "I was happier when…" Well, I wanted that back. I thought that if we could get back to our habits, then everything would be okay. If only we could just start going out again.

So, we went out to one of our favorite restaurants like we did in the good 'ole days. All I needed to do was get away. As soon as we were all loaded into the van, the emotional heaviness would be behind me, I thought. It did not go that way. On the way there, I still felt the same. My husband even made a comment about my disposition. I defended myself, but I knew that I was not acting right. I did not feel like myself. I tried to shake the dark feeling but I couldn't. Even at dinner it was still with me. I had never felt such emotional heaviness in my life. I began to feel afraid; afraid because I was realizing that the problem was not around me, it was *in* me.

It was like having a fever or a hot flash: being hot inside of your body, but feeling cool air on the surface of your skin. You know that the problem is on the inside, but you still try to change your surroundings. You just want to cool down. You ask people to open a window or turn on a fan.

I knew the problem was in me, but I still reacted like it was outside of me. At all times, the thing was there with me, so anything extra would push me over the edge. My family's actions were amplified. I had a chip on my shoulder. "Not today! I ain't the one! Don't take me there!" This was how I felt. One day I was cooking something on top of the stove and my kids were just getting on my nerves. The baby was screaming. Each kid was doing something different: talking, bickering, begging, "Look, mama, look." I was so overwhelmed and frustrated that I just walked out and sat on the porch with the spatula still in my hand. I gathered myself and walked back in to finish dinner. I thought to myself "I see why people walk out on their families or do things that are destructive." I felt like walking down the street in my house shoes, no purse, no cell phone...spatula still in hand. I just wanted peace.

What is peace? As often believed, peace does not constitute quiet or stillness, ease, or simplicity. Let us piece together some points (all pun intended):

- Peace is fruit of the spirit (Galatians 5:22).
- Jesus told the disciples that He leaves His peace with them (John 14:27).
- Jesus told the storm "peace be still" and there was calm (Mark 4:39).

What can be gathered from these points? The fruit of the spirit is produced by the Holy Ghost. So peace comes from God. Jesus said He leaves us with peace; so peace comes from God. God is eternal, unchanging, and limitless. So if we have peace from Him, then it too is eternal, unchanging, and limitless. To bring the point home, we have the peace of God. Therefore, we possess peace in all situations no matter how difficult or how changing. If this is true, then how can we see this in our lives? The answer is by faith.

When Jesus was in the boat with the disciples, they were terrified of the storm. They really believed they would die. Now, they had Jesus with them: the physical embodiment of peace. Yet, they were afraid. Why? Jesus asked "Why are ye so fearful? How is it that ye have no faith?" They had peace, but it did not manifest in their lives at that moment because they did not have faith. They were so focused on the natural that they could not see in the spirit. Jesus commanded the storm to cease and it did so immediately. He showed the disciples that He was in control all along. The question remains. What is peace?

Peace is inner calm while there is outer turmoil. Peace is conviction of God's sovereignty no matter the circumstances. The body and soul may be in crisis, but peace is drawn from the spirit. This I already knew in theory, but the Lord gave me a practical knowledge.

The scripture tells us that the enemy "cometh not but for to kill, steal and destroy (John 10:10)." He steals our peace. Now you may agree, but do you truly know how he steals your peace? Sometimes we know that the enemy is stealing something from us but don't know how he is getting it or when. He is very sly and cunning. I learned exactly how he works and now I can see it coming from afar.

Satan has lies and deception tailored just for you. If you don't know God's word at all, he may just tell you a bold lie that directly opposes the truth. If you know the word but are not very strong, then he may give you a lie that sounds very close to the truth. If you know the word and you have great confidence in God, then he will give you something different: the facts. He will present to you all of the very real and pressing issues in your life, in order to take your eyes off of Jesus, so that you will inevitably believe a lie that he didn't necessarily tell. That is deception: manipulating thoughts or actions in order to cause a person to draw a false conclusion. Oh, how the enemy was giving me the facts.

I was in the most challenging season of my life. Every day, every moment was a battle. After having my fourth child, it was the first time that I had a newborn and an infant at the same time. I am a homeschooler, so my husband being home sleeping during the day was very disruptive to my former routine. He was never able to sleep without interruptions, so he would end up taking several naps throughout the day. As a result, my help from him was never guaranteed and I was always maxed out. What really

made the pressure build was no longer having the freedom
that I once did to interact with friends and family. I was
that one who would always make it to an event unless both
of my legs were broken. I also hosted gatherings quite
often.

So now that my husband was working this night shift
eight days a week, I was missing just about everything that
anyone had and I could not have anyone over because it
was hard enough for us to get time as a family. I felt like all
of my problems were at home and I could never get away
from them. We tried to go on vacation two or three times
and each time something prevented us. I felt like a different
person. Deep down inside, I knew that the Lord was
restricting me in order to draw me to Himself.

Up until that point, I would describe myself as a pretty
constant person. I was always the same no matter what, but
I became someone else. There were times when I actually
feared for my mental health. I could begin my day feeling
fine and by noon, I didn't want to be talked to, looked at or
breathed on. What was happening to me? All the while, I
knew the truth. I knew He was with me. I just did not
understand.

I reached a point where I could empathize with people
who contemplated or committed destructive acts toward
their families: not caring anymore, walking out, adultery,
unforgiveness, becoming bitter, etc. My heart was
committed more to the Lord than it was to my escape, so I
continued to walk in the spirit. "Walk in the spirit and ye
shall not fulfill the lust of the flesh (Galatian 5:16)."

Every day was a struggle. The pain and the pressure was
so real, so great, so constant, that I began to feel
compassion for people who committed suicide. I never had
such thoughts, but for anyone to have the feelings that I had
and not have the hope of Christ, they will not long be able
to resist the whispers of the enemy to end it all. I also began
to feel compassion for the people who purposely stay away

from home or leave their families. I see them as people who need to be introduced to the Hope. They need to hear the truth and be trained in spiritual warfare. What was happening to me was not a chemical imbalance. I was under very strong demonic attack that I did not immediately recognize.

In Ephesians chapter 6, the Apostle Paul tells us to put on the whole armor of God: the belt of truth, the breastplate of righteousness, feet shod with the preparation of the gospel of peace, the shield of faith, and the sword of the spirit. Paul lived in the days when the Roman Empire was strong and thriving. Essential to Rome's continued rule was their army, which was exceptional. Besides the tactical skills that they practiced, their uniforms were the best. The careful design gave them an advantage over their enemies:

The Roman Shield

They had well-made shields that were uniquely designed to stand up to blows from weaponry, such as swords and arrows. They also used the shield to knock the enemy off of their feet then fight from behind it.

The Roman Breast Plate

They wore breastplates made of iron in order to protect the vital organs. During a battle, the opponent is looking to kill you as quickly as possible, so the aim will be for the most sensitive organs, such as the heart.

The Roman Footwear

The Roman army was well known for their exceptional footwear. A quality shoe was imperative for a soldier that would be marching for hundreds of miles. If a soldier's shoes worn out, then he was no good for battle. The

Romans wore a sandal-boot made of tough leather. Hob nails were driven through the bottom of the soul to provide a better grip, similar to that of an athlete's cleats. They had laces that went around the ankle to provide ankle support.

The Roman Belt

Soldiers wore a thick leather belt around their waist that was the center of their uniform, holding each component together. The sword sheath was made onto it. It also served as protection for their lower organs, such as the intestines and spleen.

The Roman Helmet

Perhaps, most notable is the Roman helmet. A helmet was critical to protecting the head from a blow from a weapon or even a fall to the ground. Some of the soldiers added ornaments, such as plumes and feathers.

The Roman Sword

Most importantly, they carried their sword for offense. It was vital that the sword be sharp and easily accessible. Simply having a sword was not enough to keep them alive. In order to survive on the battle field, a soldier had to know how to wield a sword. He needed to be strong, quick, and accurate for his life depended on it.

Paul was drawing a parallel and communicating that in the Lord's army, we, too, need armor. He says, "stand therefore, having your loins gird about with truth." As noted above, the belt or girdle was what held the whole uniform together.

The Girdle of Truth

Truth is what holds everything together. Truth is not synonymous with true. True is relative. "Forty degrees is cold." "I live on the right side of the street." These statements are relative. Truth is unconditional. Truth is not to be confused with facts. Facts are within truth, but outside of truth, they are without context and they become foolishness. A list of ingredients, measurements, and directions make up a recipe. Independently these things convey nothing and cannot produce a finished product.

The Truth holds the facts together. Without Truth facts have no meaning. God is the Truth. His being depends on nothing. He is unchanging. All that there is, depends on Him. Nothing can exist independently of Him for He is the context of all that there is. Without Him, everything falls apart. The Truth protects us.

The Breastplate of Righteousness

The breastplate protects two of the most vital organs: the heart and lungs. The heart pumps the blood throughout the body. The bible says in Leviticus 17:11, "For the life of the flesh is in the blood: and I have given it to you upon the altar to make an atonement for you souls: for it is the blood that maketh an atonement for the soul." As we recall, the breath of God is His Spirit.

When we are born again, we receive the breath of God and we receive a new heart. Ezekiel 36:26 says, "A new heart also will I give you, and a new spirit will I put within you: and I will take away the stony heart out of your flesh, and I will give you an heart of flesh." Through righteousness, we allow The Spirit to fully engage the heart, which is the soul, and carry out the will of the Father. We must put on the breastplate of righteousness.

Feet Shod with the Preparation of the Gospel of Peace

The word 'shod,' from the King James Version, is very important. Shod conveys that something is being carefully secured to the foot for protection, as opposed to just casually put on. Another example is how a horse is shod with shoes. A horse that will be doing a lot of walking and running is 'shod' in order to protect the hoof; excessive walking can wear the hoof down. The horseshoe is nailed to the foot of the horse to make sure that it doesn't fall off. The soldiers' shoes protected the feet from injuries and infections. A battalion could cover many different types of terrain. A good shoe made it possible to travel where it was rough, slippery, or rocky. It also helped gain leverage over the opponent. So, when they put on their footwear, they did it with purpose. They made sure that they were on right and that their feet were sufficiently supported. There was no time to keep adjusting while marching and they definitely could not afford for that shoe to come off in battle.

Gospel means simply 'good news'. The good news is that the promised redeemer has come and made a way for man to get back into fellowship with The Father. Jesus was crucified, he died, he was resurrected by The Holy Spirit, and then he ascended to heaven. The gospel carries us into territory that we otherwise could not charter. Before, we could not wage war against the kingdom of darkness. Once bound, we are now free. Adam forfeited his authority, but Jesus gained it back for us all. In Matthew 16:19, Jesus said that He has given us the keys of the kingdom of heaven. Whatsoever we bind on earth shall be bound in heaven. Whatsoever we loose on earth shall be loosed in heaven. The declaration of the gospel is what protects us from spiritual infections. Just like the hob nails, the stripes that He received gives us leverage against our opponent. His finished work on the cross and the authority that He gained upon His resurrection is what enables us to march into enemy territory and offensively attack them. It makes it possible for us to stand our ground in defense.

The Shield of Faith

Above all take the shield of faith. "Without faith it is impossible to please Him: for he that cometh to God must believe that He is, and a rewarder of them that diligently seek Him (Hebrews 11:6)." Every time the enemy strikes, we must hold up the shield of faith. When we believe God for great things, we can also use the shield of faith to knock the enemy off of his feet.

The Helmet of Salvation

Before a person is even able to fight on the battlefield against the kingdom of darkness, they must accept salvation. Salvation is the act of saving or protecting from harm. Accepting Christ as Lord and Savior is a one-time occurrence. Salvation is a process and we must choose daily to allow the word of the Lord and the guidance of His Holy Spirit to be our protection. Put on the helmet of salvation!

The Sword of the Spirit

Take the sword of the Spirit, which is the word of God. Our only means of defense is with the word of God. In order to take up the sword, we must first know it. Trying to fight in the spirit without knowing the word is like going to pull your sword and the sheath is empty. Secondly, we must believe it. Your conviction is what keeps the sword sharp. Waiving around a dull sword will get you killed. The sword has to be used quickly and with confidence or the enemy will devastate you before you have a chance to use it. The sword has to become so much a part of you that you are able to cut down your opponent before your mind finishes processing what is happening. "Casting down imaginations and every high thing that exalteth itself against the knowledge of God, and bringing into captivity every thought to the obedience of Christ (2 Corinthians 10:5)."

Praying always with all prayer and supplication in the spirit (Ephesians 6:18). Prayer is where you enter into the battlefield. First Thessalonians 5:17 tells us to pray without ceasing. In the fourth chapter of Matthew, we are given a perfect demonstration of how to use the whole armor of God:

[1]Then was Jesus led up of the Spirit into the wilderness to be tempted of the devil.
[2] And when he had fasted forty days and forty nights, he was afterward an hungered.
[3] And when the tempter came to him, he said, If thou be the Son of God, command that these stones be made bread.
[4] But he answered and said, It is written, Man shall not live by bread alone, but by every word that proceedeth out of the mouth of God.
[5] Then the devil taketh him up into the holy city, and setteth him on a pinnacle of the temple,
[6] And saith unto him, If thou be the Son of God, cast thyself down: for it is written, He shall give his angels charge concerning thee: and in their hands they shall bear thee up, lest at any time thou dash thy foot against a stone.
[7] Jesus said unto him, It is written again, Thou shalt not tempt the Lord thy God.
[8] Again, the devil taketh him up into an exceeding high mountain, and sheweth him all the kingdoms of the world, and the glory of them;
[9] And saith unto him, All these things will I give thee, if thou wilt fall down and worship me.

[10] Then saith Jesus unto him, Get thee hence, Satan: for it is written, Thou shalt worship the Lord thy God, and him only shalt thou serve.
[11] Then the devil leaveth him, and, behold, angels came and ministered unto him.

When Jesus was tempted by Satan, he had been fasting and praying. He was on the battlefield and gaining ground, so the enemy came to engage Him in combat. He tempted Him three times and Jesus won each battle. Jesus, who is The Word, wielded the sword of the Spirit with confidence. He gave an immediate response to the attacks of the enemy. He cast down each high thing that exalted itself against the knowledge of God.

When the enemy tempted Him to throw Himself down because the angels would save Him, Jesus recognized that the enemy was using a fact outside of the truth. When Jesus responded with "thou shalt not tempt the Lord thy God" he was using the belt of truth, which holds together multiple components that are useless independently. After three defensive blows, the enemy retreated. In order to war in the spirit, we must put on the whole armor of God.

Chapter 7

We Wrestle Not Against Flesh and Blood

There is more to household management than the physical aspect of work and routines. We must manage the household in the spiritual realm as well. The wife is the help meet and the keeper of the home. It is the husband's role to set a vision and lead the household as God leads Him. The wife should support the vision and defend it against all threats.

God designed woman with many special abilities that a man does not have. One of which is intuition. Webster's Dictionary defines intuition as "direct perception of truth independent of any reasoning process." Sometimes we just know things even without any logical proof. We can use this special ability to keep watch over our households.

The enemy is always trying to get into the household. When one mission is shut down, he immediately begins another. In this context, the word "enemy" refers to the Kingdom of darkness of which Satan is the chief. It is his demons that are doing the work. He is not omnipresent and he's not running around doing little jobs that don't require much power. I wanted to make that clear so that we can understand that we are dealing with real entities and not figurative speech.

There are four primary ways in which the enemy infiltrates the home. He seeks to distract, manipulate, indoctrinate, and attack. The enemy is well aware of the powerful position of the wife and mother, especially one who stays home. If he can't keep you away physically, then he will try to do so mentally.

Distraction

Media is definitely number one. At first, the only media available was printed media. Then there was the radio followed by the television. Now, we have printed media, radio broadcasts, television, and internet and the biggest one now, social media.

A great source of distraction is the cell phone. Twenty years ago it was only used for talking. Now, it compiles all other forms of media, as well as other applications that steal our attention. People call and text us and we can easily get carried away and forget our agenda for the day.

When we allow ourselves to be distracted by things like entertainment, worry, and interruptions, we miss things that we can see in the natural and we also miss what the Holy Spirit is saying. There is nothing wrong with media, entertainment, or cell phones themselves; the problem is when we allow our love for them to distract us from the presence of God so much that they become idols in our lives, and also when we used them to feed our souls filth. When the enemy sees the idols that we have in our lives, he uses that to draw us away from the Lord.

The enemy doesn't always come in scary form. Sometimes it's just a phone call that interrupts our prayer time or the time that we spend with our children.

Manipulation

The scripture describes Satan as crafty, cunning, and wise as a serpent. He is a master manipulator. The enemy manipulates our minds and emotions, or soul. He speaks to our mind in such a smooth way that we think that his words are our own thoughts. He bombards the mind with thoughts that will stir up the right emotions to evoke his desired response. Remember, the soul carries out its will through the body.

A perfect example is when an innocent person is forced to confess to a crime that they did not commit. We've all seen a crime show where the suspect is being interrogated for hours. They are exhausted, hungry, and maybe in need of the classic cigarette prop. When they first arrive, they confidently say, "I did not do this." Then the bad cop takes over. He bombards the innocent person with accusations. Then he superimposes emotions onto them. "You killed her didn't you? You hated her guts. Did she hurt your pride?" Then the person shouts out "Yes!" but they didn't really mean what they said. It's too late, they have confessed with their own mouth. This is how the enemy works. If we don't speak the word against him and command that he flee, he will continue to manipulate our souls in order to get the body to carry out his will.

When I was experiencing a season of emotional instability, my mind was actually being heavily attacked by the demonic forces. I did not immediately recognize it because I believed that they were my thoughts. I mean, the enemy wasn't coming with outlandish accusations that I could wave my hand at. He was simply magnifying negative things that were true in order to manipulate my emotions. He did much of this in my marriage. We were already going through a difficult time, so I thought that what I was thinking was coming from me. Here is an example of my train of thought:

- Kardell forgot to fix the laundry sink again.
- This is the third time I asked.
- How could anyone be so forgetful?
- Clearly it's not important to him.
- This makes my job so much more difficult.
- He doesn't forget what he wants to do.
- He must be doing this on purpose.

With each thought, my brow gets lower. My lips get tighter. Then I pick up my phone and send him a three paged text that includes words like procrastinate, initiative, and priorities. Then he gets angry because I'm sending him these texts while he's at work. His day is thrown off now because he is upset. Now, yes he should have fixed the sink and that is another book to be written about how procrastination leaves room for the enemy to come in. However, my thoughts didn't end at the sink. They became accusatory.

The enemy is an accuser of the brethren. He doesn't just accuse you. He will bring to you accusations against others. My emotions got stirred up. I was angry and irritated and itching to blow off some steam because he should have done it. Well maybe that's true, but now when he walks in the door, we're already mad at each other. Our greeting is stiff and the children are watching. Family game night has just been canceled because mommy and daddy need to talk.

Do you see how the enemy manipulates us? His goal is to get us to carry out his will. All of that could have been avoided if I forced my mouth to say, 1 Corinthians 13:4 "Charity suffereth long and is kind," followed by, "get behind me Satan." Then maybe I could have prayed and ask the Lord to speak to my husband or give me the words to speak.

Indoctrination

My grandparents' generation referred to the television as the one-eyed demon. I, myself, have even called it a portal from hell. No, the TV is not evil or from the underworld, but you better believe that it can be used to transfer energy from the kingdom of darkness. We have to be very careful about what we watch and especially what we allow our children to watch.

The enemy seeks to indoctrinate us. Demonic agendas come in all forms. They imbed the message in the lines of the cast members. They also use non-verbal subliminal messaging. If you do not protect your ear gate and eye gate, then you can become imbued with teaching from the kingdom of darkness. Seeds of sin will be planted and the right circumstances can bring forth growth. The Lord has opened up my eyes to the tactics of the enemy through TV and movies, and now I see things clearly.

One way that the enemy ropes you in is with the classic bait and switch. After you get comfortable with something and don't want to part with it, then here comes the agenda. There was one show that I absolutely loved. It was a show about a woman who had stood by her husband…I'll just say it. The show was called *The Good Wife*. I got in on season one of the show. The plot was about a woman who stayed with her politician husband after learning of his adulterous and political scandals that landed him in prison. All this on the backdrop of law and politics, and I love my law and politics shows. Despite the destruction and shame that he brought onto the family, she continued to fight for their marriage. Once a stay at home mom, she picked her career back up as a defense attorney to provide for the family while her husband was locked up. A good wife, right?

In the following season, the good wife was changing. She was gaining momentum in her career. She was no longer walking in shame. With her husband away, she was learning some things about herself. She was being reminded of some things that she had forgotten, like her college boyfriend who was now her boss. At first, she showed no interest in him, but slowly she began to reassess. She began to wonder if she should even stay with her husband. I mean, he did some terrible things and he was in prison. She didn't jump into a relationship. It was more like catching an eye here and there, staying late at the office, "would you like to get take-out?" sort of thing. She was really struggling with whether she should re-visit this old flame.

Well, she must not have heard the Lord when he spoke because I heard "Thou shalt not commit adultery." That was it, I couldn't watch the show anymore and boy did I wanna. It took about a month for me to get over it, too. I never watched the show again, but from the previews, I gathered that she became adulterous. I also noticed that the series cover went from a picture of a solemn-faced woman dressed in black and standing behind her husband, to a woman in a crimson red dress sitting alone and in a provocative manner. I doubt that the color represented the blood of Jesus. One of the cover photos even showed her standing between her husband and boyfriend and holding both their hands.

That show was a perfect way of indoctrinating. God said, "Thou shall not commit adultery" and the show said, "It's complicated." Every word and every scene was a seed being sowed, and surely the enemy intended to come back and water it. The same holds true for children's television programs and books, too. No matter how colorful they are, if they go against the word of God, seem a little off, or even if you just aren't sure, turn it off. We must protect them from the wiles of the devil. We cannot allow our children to be indoctrinated because it keeps them occupied. We cannot allow their minds to be filled with darkness because it's their favorite show. Many times I was heart-broken when I had to tell my children "Turn it off." The way I avoided that was by taking a lead approach. I told them which shows they *were* allowed to watch and that was it. Any new show had to be pre-screened and approved. I was always listening closely to the shows. On one occasion, I was washing dishes in the kitchen and I heard a cartoon say follow your heart and believe in yourself. I immediately went to the living room and said, "Don't believe in yourself; believe in Christ, and don't follow your heart, because the heart is deceitful above all things and desperately wicked." I plucked that seed right out of the ground.

Our children understand that there is a tug of war going on for their souls. They are learning to identify the crafts of the enemy themselves and sometimes make up their own minds that they do not want to partake. It's not about shielding them and pretending like evil doesn't exist. It's about shielding them until they learn how to shield themselves. Cover the eye and ear gates until they decide to cover it themselves. Statements like "You can't shelter your children" are absolute foolishness. The military shelters and trains before sending troops into battle, but the people of God are called fanatics when they shelter their young ones. If you don't shelter your children, you are not doing your job. Watch over their souls.

When Zoey was about four years old, she brought me her Minnie Mouse coloring book and said that she didn't think she should have it because it was inappropriate. Confused, I asked her why and she said because Minnie Mouse was trying to be sexy. I was blown away. She flipped through the pages and showed how Minnie Mouse was posing and lowering her eyes in a provocative way. I looked at the pages and she was definitely being sensual, but I guess I just waved my hand at it because it was sweet little Minnie. I said, "Okay. Zoey, you show me which pages you think you shouldn't have and you can tear them out." When she was done, there were only about three pages left. Because Zoey had a foundation, she was able to see with her own spiritual eye and make her own judgement even at four-years-old.

Music is by far the most powerful medium of indoctrination. That is Satan's specialty, for he was the chief musician in heaven. When you sing a song, you are speaking into your own soul. That's why it's so sad to hear a child singing filth, totally unaware of the meaning. The power of life and death is in the tongue. Godly music will usher in the presence of God. This we know. So we cannot pretend that ungodly music does not usher in the presence of the demonic. The enemy can couple a beautiful sound with the most destructive lyrics. The beauty of music will cause a person to passively accept that which they never would apart from a tune.

Music that was originally written for an adult audience is now being used in children's movies. Was Prince's music appropriate for children? When I heard "You don't have to be beautiful to turn me on" coming from my TV, movie night was over. Many people think that's no big deal. It's just a song, right? Then, when their child has sex out of wedlock, they don't know what happened. Kids don't decide things like that overnight. Seeds are planted, watered, and cultivated. Parents must take the sword of the spirit, pluck seeds out, and cut branches down. No, we can't get everything, but we should try.

If we have pests in our home, do we say "We can't get all of them" or do we aim to eradicate? If you do not want pests in the first place, keep a clean house. Do not create an environment that attracts them. If you want to make your fight against the kingdom of darkness a bit easier, do not make your home a place where demons are welcome. Pay attention to media agendas. If it's not of God, turn it off or throw it away.

Attack

When the devil sees that you refuse to be distracted, you will not allow him to manipulate you, and you shut your ears to indoctrination, he will just attack you. The enemy is not all powerful like God. He is limited, so he must be efficient. He uses no more force than necessary. So, he will only attack you if he sees that you are going after God and coming for the kingdom of darkness. The enemy may send outsiders to bring harm to us or he may try to divide the house from the inside, just like he did in the Garden of Eden.

We know better than Eve now. We have the promised Redeemer and the promise of the Holy Spirit. We also have God's written word. So, we have to do better. As household managers, we must open our eyes to the spirit realm. Pray offensively as well as defensively. Use your natural intuitive abilities and listen to the voice of Holy Spirit. Bind up the hand of the enemy against your children as well as your husband. Be very aware that the enemy may seek to use your children against the family. What he wants the most is to cut off the head of the family: the husband.

Protect your husband's vision even if the enemy is using him to destroy it. Protect the vision of your husband even if he has yet to realize it. "We wrestle not against flesh and blood, but against principalities, against powers, against the rulers of the darkness of this world, against spiritual wickedness in high places (Ephesians 6:12)." It is imperative to recognize that the enemy operates through people. So no matter what evil a person does, it can be dealt with in prayer. Spiritual warfare is a full-time job that should never be taken lightly. Everyone needs to be on their assigned watch tower.

The Holy Spirit gives us to know when the enemy is attacking us. You don't always blame the enemy for sickness, but maybe one particular time you knew that he was involved. Children cry and scream quite a bit, but sometimes you know that it is a spiritual attack.

I remember when Zoey was two years old, she went through a phase where she would wake up screaming every night around 3:00 a.m. She would be completely out of control: kicking and screaming. I thought that maybe she was in pain or something. When I would ask her what was wrong, she would never say. Eventually, I recognized that this was a spiritual attack. At the time, my husband was working the midnight shift, so I was home alone. When the enemy sees that the wife is alone, he will definitely try to wreak havoc. Every night I would be so frustrated and then I would wake up tired. One particular night, I was fed up and I rebuked the demonic attack. I laid my hands on Zoey and prayed for her. She stopped waking up in a tantrum. The enemy needed to be chased away by the authority of Jesus.

We have to fight the kingdom of darkness, but we must occupy the territory as well. We must first do this inwardly by focusing on Christ. We occupy the territory by inviting the Holy Spirit into our homes. Acknowledge Him at the beginning of the day. Give offerings of praise and adoration. Let the atmosphere be saturated with worship music and the word of God. Create an atmosphere that will welcome the presence of God and make devils flee.

Chapter 8

Dreams, Identity & Purpose.

Many women serve in their homes faithfully, but in the back of their minds, they slowly let go of their dreams. Time is ticking and they simply cannot see the possibility of achieving their goals and raising a family at the same time. So, they slowly let their dreams fade away, and may even feel that they have done God and their family a favor. This is a tragedy. When we submit ourselves to Christ, we are giving Him everything. We cannot separate what we want from what He wants. He gives us the talents and abilities and all of our dreams and passions stem from what He put within us. They will all serve under our purpose.

He gives us this unique opportunity to bring Him glory while allowing us to get satisfaction. Women of God, The Lord has great purpose for each and every one of our lives. We have been lied to/duped/hoodwinked into believing that our husbands, our children, and our household duties are quenching our passions, hindering us from our goals, and swallowing up our identities. That is a lie from the pit of hell! Do not allow the enemy to convince you that your role as a wife and mother is not connected to the passions that the Lord put in you! You are not gifted of yourself. So would not He, who created you, also cultivate in you the gift that He gave you for His own purpose? Please believe Him. In His timing, He will birth a great work in you.

Giving birth means not only delivering your own blessing, but also a blessing for the world. The natural way to deliver a baby involves intense pain. The contractions will force you out of your comfort zone and literally open you up wide enough to allow the baby to come down the canal. If you have ever experienced labor pain then you can relate.

At some point in your pregnancy, you think of the pain that will come during delivery. It scares you a bit or a lot. At the end of pregnancy, you to deliver. You are so tired that you welcome the pain. You constantly look for any signs of labor. "Today? Nope. How about now? Nope." Then it happens. Your water may break. The pain may start off very slight and faint. You aren't quite sure if it's real labor yet. When it intensifies, you know that it's real. You alert others.

You are in pain, but not yet enough pain to act out. You don't want to be over dramatic. The contractions come faster and last longer. Now it hurts enough for you to employ breathing techniques. You are trying to manage the pain but you are still conscious of people watching you. You're still trying to be polite and cooperative. You are so close to the prize of a brand new baby, but it's so difficult that you regret rushing your delivery or even, ever becoming pregnant.

You're still holding onto your dignity. Then it hits you. That moment when the pain has reached a level where you are so desperate to deliver that you will do anything to end the pain. You are no longer focused on anyone around you. You couldn't care less about what they think. You open your legs as wide as you can. You don't care who looks. You are in a position that is so raw, so vulnerable, and so intimate. You bear down, and with every muscle in your body you push that baby out. There's no turning back. If you want that baby, if you want the pain to stop, you push hard. The head begins to crown and you are motivated to endure a little longer. When that baby comes out, it's the greatest feeling of relief ever. The pain is instantly gone and you are suddenly overjoyed. Then the memory of the pain slowly fades away as your child grows up and blesses you, your family, and the world. It was so worth it.

We are all pregnant with gifts, talents, ministries, and purposes from the Lord. In order to deliver what He has ordained for your life, you must allow it to grow and He determines what is necessary for growth. He will determine when you are ready to deliver. We will discuss this further later.

When the Lord is ready to deliver His purpose for your life, the experience is quite similar to delivering a child. You have your dreams and desires, your ideas and your passions. You are excited about launching into the world, although you have some fears of change, rejection, and failure.

When He is ready for you to begin your work, you will be uncomfortable. By uncomfortable, I mean your life will be upside down. You will experience great pain. You will ask "Lord Why?" This is the beginning of labor. He will give you breaks in between contractions, but the waves of pain will get closer and closer together. You will be humbled, tested, strengthened, and you will grow. Your life will be so difficult that you will need to press into Him to resist your flesh and maintain your sanity. He will not let you go no matter what.

Now your fears are turning into regret. "Why did I pray for this?" Like the children of Israel, you will long to go back to Egypt even though you know that what is ahead of you is so much greater. Even with a great promise ahead of you, you are not sure that you can endure until the end.

The scripture says in 2 Corinthians 12:9, "My grace is sufficient for thee: for my strength is made perfect in weakness." This is a critical turning point at which you are ready to submit to God fully. Your cervix is fully dilated and you are ready to push. Oh, when it is time to push, you are no longer captured by fear. The pain is so great that you are ready to do whatever it takes to make it stop. You no longer care what people think. You are convinced that you can do all things through Christ which strengthens you, as stated in Philippians 4:13.

So, you bear down and you push that thing out. You walk by faith and not by sight. The Lord gives you to know that you are close to birthing what He put in you. People see your gift crowning and they tell you what they see the Lord bringing forth. You then get excited and more confident because you are close to the end. You can't see what's happening, but you can sure feel it.

When the fruit comes out, there will be excitement, but you are not done. It's so close, but there is more in you that has to come out. You push, and push, and push, until you fully deliver what God has impregnated you with. The pain stops immediately because His will has just been translated into the earth. You have just transitioned from pregnancy to parenting. Now it is time to learn how to nurture what He has given you dominion over.

We must be careful not to attempt to parent what the Lord has birthed in us on our own. God is working through us, so in order to be effective, we have to remain in fellowship with Him and follow His lead. As soon as we pull away from Him, we are trying to manage what He gave us in our own might. This can be destructive to our own lives, as well as to the ministry.

When our prayer life weakens and we are not seeking Him diligently in the word, the ideas stop, the fiery passion is extinguished, and we no longer have the grace to endure. In order to operate at optimal level, we must stay as close as possible to the Lord.

Think of an old cordless phone. As long as you remain within a certain range of the base, the reception is good. As you get further from the base, it becomes increasingly difficult to hear. At a certain point, the call will be dropped. You can't just take that last step back to continue the call. You have to get back in range and then redial. Even if you do stay in range, you can only use the phone for so long before you have to return it to the base to be recharged. The phone will not shut off without warning. You can look at the display screen to check the battery power. In addition to the battery display, the phone will give off low battery warning sounds. If you wait until the phone is completely dead to charge it, then you will have to leave it on the base for a while before you can use it again. This is exactly how it works when the Lord gives us a work. We need to be with him in order to be effective and we need to step back from our work and be refilled.

Imagine you allow your toddler to play with your cell phone or tablet. They get wrapped up in a game and then they walk away with your device. You say, "Oh no. If you want to use this, you have to stay right here." You want to make sure that your hardware is not damaged or that nothing gets deleted. If the child protests or is disobedient, then you say, "Fine. You can't have it then."

The take home lesson is that whatever the Lord has purposed for our lives is of extreme importance. It is not just for us nor is it just about us. It involves the lives of many and will have a tremendous impact. Most importantly, it is about His glory being revealed. We are fallen beings with corrupt souls and bodies, so fragile that we are one uncovered cough away from being sick for a week. There is no way that we could handle God's business on our own.

I have heard women say that when they stayed home, they felt like they were losing themselves. They went to work not just because they needed the money, but because they wanted to maintain some sense of identity. This is a poor basis for such a major decision. There is no doubt that the responsibilities in the home are tremendous: requiring a great amount of time and energy. A decision for a wife to work outside of the home should be made with the good of the entire household in mind. The basis of this decision has to be rooted in wisdom and truth.

The truth is identity is not what you do. It is who you are. Our identities cannot be found in our careers or accomplishments. We do not create or maintain our identities. We come into the realization of who we are. No matter where we are or what we have in life, our identities remain the same. A chimpanzee is a wild animal whether in the jungle or in a suit. If you feel lost or like you are fading, then you need a better understanding of identity.

If you have accepted Jesus as your Lord and savior, then your identity is in Him. Galatians 3:27 says, for all of you who were baptized in Christ have clothed yourselves with Christ. The Lord God tells the prophet Jeremiah, "Before I formed thee in the belly, I knew thee (Jeremiah 1:5)." All that you are is in Him. Therefore, the only possible way to walk in your purpose is through obedience to Him. There are no alternatives.

So, as a wife, mother, and household manager, you must believe that doing laundry; cooking; giving your husband sex; and nurturing children is doing the work of the Lord, as well as impacting the world.

Being faithful to your family shows the Lord that you can obey. Yes, Lord, when I'm tired. Yes, Lord, when I don't wanna. Yes, Lord, when I feel unappreciated. Yes, Lord, when I'm angry. Yes, Lord, when I don't see the connection. When you reach a point where you are willing to give up your dreams in order to give yourself fully to the Lord and your primary responsibility, it is then that you are ready to receive promotion. He will make your dreams come true in a greater way than you imagined.

For years I would brainstorm about how I could start a business while raising small children. I would have so many ideas, but it was like there was nothing that I could do with them. I felt inadequate, left behind, and dull. I loved being a wife and mother, but I felt like had a lot more in me than the same cook, clean, and correct routine. I came to a point where I gave up trying to plan my life. I decided to be content and focus on my family. As for my entrepreneurial endeavors, I just put it in the hands of the Lord. At that point, the Lord began to move in my life because I had finally given up control. I finally stopped trying to plan my life out. I decided to be faithful to the present assignment and allow the Lord to unfold my life. I became increasingly submitted, desiring only for my life what God ordained.

My oldest daughter has tried to be a woman since she was born. I have spent years trying to hold her back and convince her to slow down. She wanted to wear nail polish, lip gloss, and clothing that was too old for her. She wanted to wear several pieces of jewelry at one time. When I saw that she was unsatisfied with looking like a little kid, I took everything away from her. She was no longer allowed to wear any jewelry at all. I was not moved by complaining or begging. After a while, when I saw that she was content and making herself look nice with what she had, it was then that I decided to allow her to have the things back. Not only did her attitude release to her what she desired, but it allowed me to bless her with the things that I wanted her to have.

In her mind, I was mean old mama that didn't want her to have anything, but the truth was that I actually wanted her to have more than she imagined. I looked forward to taking her to girly stores and getting what I liked for her, as well as what she wanted. To do that before her heart was ready would be doing her an injustice. The impurities that were in her heart would only grow and branch out into other areas of her life. When she turned nine, I took her to the mall and did what I dreamed to do. She got more than she imagined. She may have thought that I changed. Nope, mama didn't change. Sweetheart, you changed. This is exactly how God deals with us.

While you serve diligently and wait on God's timing to launch you into His work for your life, cultivate your talents and gifts. You may desire to do ministry work, start a company, or travel the world. Perhaps you are into fashion or saving animals. It does not matter. Prepare for what you say that you want. Prepare like you believe your prayers will be answered.

- Learn God's word and the applications for your own life
- Establish a strong prayer life.
- Practice giving thanks in all things.
- Invest in books, audio materials, and programs that are related to your dreams.
- Write down your ideas.
- Practice your work within the boundaries that God allows.
- Surround yourself with people who will encourage you to embrace God's timing.
- Write down the things that you would like to do.
- Express your desires to the Lord.
- Talk about your desires to people.

⟩   Practice being a good manager of money and
     resources.
⟩   Practice being a timely person.

My father told me many times, "You have a book in you
and I believe you will teach women." I thought to myself,
"Not quite a book. Maybe a pamphlet." I began to write
down the things that the Lord would drop in my spirit. He
would give me full quotes that I knew I was not smart
enough to come up with on my own. I wrote down each
one. There was no context. I just kept writing them.

A few years later, I met a woman in the grocery store
while shopping with my four kids. She was shopping with
her husband and two kids. She approached me so boldly
that I thought that I knew her. I knew I had never seen her
before, but there was some familiarity there. She was in
awe that I was shopping with so many kids, alone. I had no
choice as my husband's work schedule always forced me
to. She was so kind and bubbly. She told me that they were
visiting from California. As I smiled and talked, I was
thinking to myself "Who is this woman? Why is she so
interested in me?" When she asked to exchange numbers I
said, "Lord what are you up to?" It was clear to me that the
Lord had sent her, but I didn't know why.

When we talked on the phone for the first time, it was a
slow conversation at first. I was still trying to figure out
what her mission was. I asked her if she was a Christian
and she confirmed. I knew it. That's why I felt like I knew
her. As we learned more about each other, the conversation
picked up. She found out that I was a homeschooler and the
conversation exploded because she was considering home
educating her children. We talked about child-rearing,
cooking, and overall household management. She found
wisdom in the things that I was saying and guess what she
said? "You have a book in you." Bingo! Just like that, the
Lord revealed the reason for our encounter. I got so excited.

It turned out that she was a new author and had just published a book. She told me to begin writing immediately. I took heed and began that day, as I knew that the Lord had sent her.

That distant dream was suddenly in my face. I pulled out all of those thoughts that I had written over the years and began to assemble them. I stood back and allowed the Lord to determine when my time was to fulfill some of my dreams, and He brought it to fruition way before I expected. When the Lord started moving, He started moving quickly.

I have a culinary arts degree and cooking is my passion. People frequently ask me for advice on foods or cooking techniques. I get really excited to share it. One day, someone in a class overheard me talking to someone about food and they said "you should do classes." Many people had said that to me before, but this time was different. This time I really heard them. I said to myself, "Duhh teach classes." I began to write down ideas in my notebook. On Thanksgiving, my cousin asked me what I would charge to do an in-home cooking demonstration for a group of friends. I couldn't believe it. I went to my room and got my notebook to show her that I had just written that idea down. It was certainly clear now that the Lord was sending people to direct me. I took the clues.

Two months later, I was at a birthday party at our friends' house. Another friend asked me when would I finish culinary school. I said, "oh, I graduated years ago." He said "oh, I didn't know." He then began to ask me about my business ideas. I told him about my new idea to teach cooking classes. He got excited because he is a small business coach. He was trying to make my idea an immediate reality. He said you need to establish yourself as an authority in your field by writing a book. I checked out when he said that. I thought, "Write a book about what?" Besides, I had just started this book and I thought surely the

Lord wouldn't have me start another project. That would be too much. He asked when I planned to start. I said in about five years. He said, "Ha! You mean five weeks?" I explained that I had four little kids and one was nursing. He was not trying to hear it. I said, "Ian, you're crazy." He told me to watch a video of a presentation that he had given so that I would get another perspective on business. I watched the video that night and that night I decided that I was ready to start a business. I couldn't believe it. The Lord sent him as well. He became my business coach and we got started right away. I was sure that the Lord told me to write this book. Now he was telling me to start a business. I wondered if I was hearing Him correctly. I did not want to do anything in my own might.

One of the things that I wanted to do was make worksheets for my clients to show, on paper, exactly what I was teaching. I began what I intended to be a three-page document and I couldn't stop writing. I had more than I thought. That three-page document became a publication. I titled it, *Great Cooks Kitchen Efficiency Manual*. I published it and launched the business before I even finished this book. Just months prior, when Ian said write a book to establish myself as an authority, I thought the idea was far-fetched. I thought, "Lord, what is going on? Why would you have me doing so many things at once?" Later on I had an idea to solve the problem of food access in the city of Detroit. I knew it was from the Lord because I know I could not have come up with it on my own. I simply wrote it down but had no plan. I thought it would make a good non-profit organization. A few months later, my sister told me that she was in a grant writing class that was free. She offered for me to sign up. I wasn't all that interested, so I dragged my feet to sign up. When I had trouble enrolling, I didn't press any further. She followed up and encouraged me to try again. The class was free and close to my house, so I said "why not?" On day one, I was ready to drop out of the class. The instructor wanted everyone to share the name of their non-profit and the mission. That was not what I had signed up for. I was just there to sit in the back, take some notes, and store the information for later use. I remained in the class. Again, it was free, close to home, and my sister was in it with me.

So, I was now forced to develop the idea that I had. I came up with a name and brainstormed about potential board members. Just like that, I was starting a non-profit. My head was spinning. I had to remain very close to the Lord because there was just way too much going on at once. The last thing I wanted was to take on a task that was outside of His will. After much prayer, I decided that it was, in fact, the Lord that was leading me. In fact, He was pushing me into everything.

If you are like me, then you tend to think that God moves slowly. Almost like He just wants to make you wait. So, when things move quickly and you get overwhelmed, you feel like it may not be the Lord. The scripture speaks a lot about waiting on the Lord. As believers, we constantly remind each other to wait on the Lord. However, sometimes we're not waiting on the Lord, but rather He is waiting on us. The Lord waits for us to submit to Him. He waits on us to seek Him. He waits on us to put our trust in Him. He waits for us to properly manage what He has already given us. When we finally position ourselves in His will and become still, it is then that He will open the flood gates and blessings will overwhelm our lives.

God is timeless so His will is not confined to our time. What does this mean? We cannot assume that the Lord will wait until a certain age or phase of our lives to bring us into our purpose. So for the stay-at-home mother who dreams of recording music, do not assume that the Lord is waiting until your children reach a certain age. If you feel that you are purposed to travel the world, do not make your mind up that you have to wait until your children graduate or you reach retirement. We are finite beings, so it is natural that we yield to such challenges. Thankfully, we serve a God who has no limits. So we need only to obey His word, serve Him diligently, and make our requests known unto Him. Do these things with expectation and watch Him give you much more than what you asked for or imagined.

Do not allow housework or outside work to quench your passions. You must make time to prepare for your purpose. If you can watch TV for an hour, you can brainstorm for an hour. Be honest with yourself about how you are spending your time.

> Do not allow housework or outside work to quench your passions. You must make time to prepare for you purpose.

The above actions are those of a servant who is faithful, diligent, responsible, and prepared. Do this and God will reward your faithfulness with more than you asked for. These things I know not in theory, but through experience; for it is how God molded me to write these very words to you.

One of my favorite passages in the bible is Hebrews chapter eleven. It is what we called the Faith Hall of Fame. When you read that chapter, you can't help but grow in excitement and maybe shout hallelujah at the end. The chapter opens up with "Now faith is the substance of things hoped for and evidence of things not seen." So, in the context of your dreams and aspirations, faith will be the driving force, the vehicle by which you will arrive at your destination. Due to the extreme dilution of the word faith, I must expound on what faith is and also talk about what it is not.

Faith is not the same as a wish. A wish is a desire, without expectation, that requires no action on the part of the recipient. Faith is an expectation based on a promise, a guarantee, or some prior knowledge or experience. With faith, the recipient will take some kind of action because they are confident that they will get a return on their actions. James 2:26 says, "For as the body without the spirit is dead, so faith without works is dead also." This scripture lets us know that we can't make a wish and call it faith. So if we die with our God given passions within us and having never lived in our purpose, then we have only ourselves to blame. Not God. Not our circumstances.

How does a wife and mother have faith that the Lord will make a way for her to live out the purpose that He gave her? Follow these principles in this order.

Submit to God

It is the Lord that created us. It is He that has given us purpose and in order to live fully in it, we must seek Him and submit to Him. When we submit to God, we can distinguish our godly dreams from lustful dreams. We do not want to waste time praying or waiting for something that is outside of the will of God. A person who is not submitted to God may, to an extent, have the chance to operate in what God has purposed for their lives. However, in order to be totally fulfilled, one must be in fellowship with Him. Our full purpose is in the mind of God and without a connection to Him, it is impossible to know what we should be doing and impossible to do it. Living fully in our purpose requires His wisdom and power as well.

Most people don't read the owner's manual to a new cell phone. We all feel like we know how cell phones work. They seem to be pretty much the same. You may have your phone for a while and eventually feel like you know the ins and outs. I guarantee that if you read the manual, you will find some information that you did not know, something that your phone can do that will surprise you. The full purpose of the phone is in the mind of the creator. In order to get the maximum benefit from the device, you must read the manual. It is there that the creator will tell you all that the phone is capable of, as well as well as show you the commands to get the results.

Serve Him diligently

Serving God should not be separate from our dreams. We do not trade off with the Lord. It's not, "I'll do what you want then you give me what I want." That attitude shows a lack of understanding of who God is. God is not a selfish God. He did not create us to serve Him and we not have any satisfaction in life. We can look at creation and tell that He really wants us to enjoy life. He put in us the desire for great things. God is not a man. We don't work out deals with Him. He is Alpha and Omega and we are dust that breathe His breath.

Our purpose is to worship and serve the Lord. He made each one of us to worship and serve Him differently. Now, we all worship and serve Him in the manner that He has commanded in His word, but in or own unique way. It is within our purpose that we live our dreams. For example, you may dream of traveling the world. God may have put this desire in you because His purpose is for you to carry the gospel to the nations. You may dream of being a hairstylist. God gave you that desire because the people that you are called to reach can be found in a hair salon.

We must not separate our lives into compartments and mark them "ministry, dreams, work, etc." We must offer our full lives "a living sacrifice, holy, acceptable unto God, which is [our] reasonable service (Romans 12:1)." Then, the Lord will take it and make it into what He wants it to be, which will in turn be much more than we desired for ourselves.

So, as you raise your small children, do not count down the days until the last child leaves the home so that you can pursue your aspirations. Have faith that your current work is, in fact, ministry to God and is getting you closer to those dreams.

As wives and mothers, our first responsibility is to our family. Your home ministry can serve as an indicator of how ready you are to do anything else. If you are wondering how close you are, think of what your actions and attitudes are expressing to God.

> ⸙ Complaining about how much housework you have to do:
>> Lord, if I can't handle these dishes, surely I can't run a business.

> ⸙ Serving with a hard heart:
>> Dear, Jesus, I'm not ready to go out into the world to serve. I don't even want to serve my family.

> ⸙ Failing to invest into your children:
>> God, I cannot pour into anything else because I have not given enough to my children yet.

> ⸙ Refusing to submit to your husband:
>> Lord it's really you that I won't submit to.

When we look at it this way, it's no wonder that our dreams are dying. They are being choked out by bitterness, entitlement, laziness, immaturity, disobedience, and ungratefulness. The Lord cannot cultivate the seed that He placed within you because the soil of your soul is unfertile. Fertile soil contains joy, humility, diligence, endurance, obedience, and thanksgiving.

Zahria (my oldest child) wants to be a fashion designer. In her young mind, all she needs to know how to do is draw cute clothes. I frequently have to remind her of the many things that she must know in order to fulfill this goal. She will need to learn how to draw the human figure, be proficient in measurements in both the Imperial system (used in the United States) and the Metric System, have great communications skills, organizational skills, marketing skills, and many other abilities that would make it possible to be a successful fashion designer. None of that sounds fun to her or relevant to what she wants to do, but it is all necessary. She wants to just skip to fabrics and colors.

Likewise, wives and mothers can be the same. We don't see how potty-training and cooking dinner is contributing to our dreams. How will endless laundry lead to my fulfillment? We must realize that the Lord uses all of our life experiences to carry us into His calling on or lives. Potty-training teaches patience, grace, and mercy. Cooking dinner teaches us creativity and coordination. That endless laundry will teach you service and endurance. It will also build you some muscle.

Our roles as mothers and wives are not separate from our individual purposes. When we come to believe that all aspects and experiences work together for our good, then we will throw ourselves fully into our assignments and work diligently to please the Lord. If we cannot faithfully serve the ones that we love the most, then we cannot expect the Lord to send us out to serve anyone else nor can we expect to be served ourselves. There is a direct increasing relationship between how well we serve our household and how much of our dreams we will get to live.

In Matthew chapter 16, Jesus tells the disciples what is required to follow him. He says:

24 If any man will come after me, let him deny himself, and take up his cross and follow me.

25 For whosoever will save his life shall lose it: and whosoever will lose his life for my sake shall find it.
26 For what is a man profited, if he shall gain the whole world and lose his own soul? Or what shall a man give in exchange for his soul.

How does this passage apply to wives and mothers? When we get married and have children, ready or not, we enter into a ministry. Once we enter this ministry, we are now responsible for it. God will judge us based on our works and our level of dedication. We can no longer put ourselves first. That means that all of our decisions have to be based on what is best for everyone. If you try to put yourself first and hold on to your desires without regard to how it impacts your family, you will cheat yourself out of blessings. If you deny yourself by only going in a direction that is best for the family, you will be blessed greatly with more than what you wanted. What does a woman profit if she "has it all," but her household is falling apart? What will a woman give in exchange for her family? Money? Prestige? Pleasure? Our children's hearts need to be shepherded and our husbands need spiritual defense through prayer. Our job description entails much more than meal service, bedtime routines, sex, and date nights.

Make your requests known

When we are submitted to the Lord, our will becomes one with His will. More and more, we want what He wants for our lives. We seek to please Him. God does not seek to please us, but he does desire that we experience life as He intended. That is, life abundantly. We obtain what belongs to us two ways: we ask and we fight for it. We live in a fallen world where the enemy has stolen all that God intended for us, so we must obtain what already belongs to us. One way in which we get what we want is by asking.

Our fellowship with God was broken after Adam sinned. Before corruption, there was no need to ask for anything. God had provided everything already. There was no lack. Disobedience to God was a forfeiture of all that He gave man. Satan came in and claimed what Adam gave up. Jesus died in order to cover our sins and also so that we could have back what the enemy stole. So, we shouldn't have to ask for anything, right? Wrong. If you have accepted Christ as Lord, you are a new creature; however, you still inhabit the same sinful flesh. Here is the point. We must ask for things because if the Lord gave it without us asking, we would give the credit to ourselves, something or someone else. God wants the glory. Thus, if you receive by asking, there will be no denying that He provided. Asking keeps us humbled. Consider the following verses:

> *John 16:23 And in that day ye shall ask me nothing. Verily, verily, I say unto you, whatsoever ye shall ask the Father in my name, he will give it you. 24 Hitherto ye have asked nothing in my name: ask, and ye shall receive, that your joy may be full.*
> *James 4:3 Ye ask and receive not, because ye ask amiss, that ye may consume it upon your lusts.*

We must also fight for what God has already given to us. The enemy has taken into possession many things that the Lord has ordained for us to have. This is not just in reference to material things, such as houses, vehicles, and luxury items. The enemy steals those things as well, but we often put too much emphasis on physical possessions that stem from our spiritual blessings. Even more devastating is when the enemy steals our joy, peace, time, focus, confidence and faith, to name a few. When he has those things, we are rendered sorrowful, distressed, distracted, fearful, and doubtful. These are the tactics that he uses to stop us from operating in our God-given purposes, receiving blessings, and living life abundantly so The Lord will get the glory.

The Lord has taken back all power and authority through his blood sacrifice on the cross. He has given us the power necessary through the gift of the Holy Spirit, and He has provided for us instructions and encouragement through His written word. We have been equipped for battle. So, in order to obtain what belongs to us, we must take it by force.

Taking everything back by force is a tough battle, but it has been spelled out for us in the word. Remain obedient to Christ, seek Him diligently, and trust in His word no matter the circumstance. That is all to it. It is simple, but it is a war with increasingly difficult battles. There will be highs and lows. Sometimes it may become so difficult that you re-evaluate whether you want to continue, but you must hold fast to Christ because there is no rest outside of Him. All things that are good are in Him. All things that matter are in Him. So, turning away from Him when you are weary is like taking a break from running from a bear. You would be consumed. So, keep running.

Prepare for what you pray for.

"But without faith it is impossible to please Him: for he that cometh to God must believe that he is, and that he is a rewarder of them that diligently seek Him (Hebrews 11:6)." This scripture tells us that no matter what we ask of the Lord, if we do not have faith, He will not move on our behalf. So how do we exhibit faith that God will bring us into our purpose and make our godly dreams come true? We prepare for what we pray for. We prepare for what we say we want.

Preparation is an act of faith. You prepare because you have expectation. Your level of preparation will be directly correlated with the amount of confidence you have. You probably know of a person whose word is not worth very much. They may be dishonest or just flaky. If that person tells you that they will pick you up to take you somewhere, you will be careful of how much time and effort you put into being ready. You won't even begin to mentally prepare until the day is closer. Maybe you won't choose your best outfit. You'll probably still plan to watch your favorite TV show because you don't really believe that they are coming. Then when the call or text and says, "I'm on my way," you rush to get ready. Even though you have had ample time, you are not prepared. You did not have expectation. Now if, a person who you have confidence in tells you the same thing, you will be on the curb. You know they mean what they say, so you don't want to waste their time. How much more should we prepare for the Lord's work? God is not a man that He shall lie and nothing can stop Him from doing what He said. So if you ask Him to do something, your due diligence is to prepare for the blessing.

How do you prepare for your dreams? Invest your time and money into your dreams. Your calendar and your bank statement will testify of your faith. Whatever talents that God has placed in you, cultivate them.

Learn

Research, read books, take classes, attend speaking engagements, hire a coach, or talk to someone who has been successful in the field you are going in.

You can't make it solely on anointing. Just because the Lord placed a burning passion in your heart and people recognize it, does not mean that you are ready. The Lord wants His people to be skilled and experienced. Do not allow pride and ignorance to launch you prematurely and be your demise. The purpose is to bring God glory, so you must show yourself worthy.

Practice

Again, anointing is not synonymous with skillfulness. God may have called you to do something, but in order to do it well, we must practice. If the Lord has given you to be a visual artist, no matter how good you are, do not elevate yourself above further training. If the Lord has called you to the mission field, it would do you well to study culture of the people that you are called to serve. God gets the glory out of what we do when people see good results. However, we must also consider how much more glory we bring Him when we are humble and diligent.

When the world sees that we, too, have paid our dues, they will marvel at our character. They will respect us and know that we have a divine calling on our lives. There will be no need for others to elevate us or for us to elevate ourselves. God will elevate us, that He may be glorified.

Invest money

We live in a world where we need money or something of value to get what we need. We cannot wait for the day that the Lord will rain down what we need in order to achieve our dreams. We must use what He has given us. No matter how little you have, you have something. When the Lord sees that you are a faithful servant over a little, He will give more. If you are called to the mission field abroad, you may not yet have the money to travel, but maybe you can afford a $15.00 book on missionary work in a foreign land. You must value your dream above a cup of coffee or a movie ticket. Of course you can still enjoy luxuries, but you cannot say that you are waiting on the Lord to provide the money that you need when you are spending it on other things. The Lord dispenses resources as we need them and as we exhaust yesterday's provision.

For many years, I dreamed big about what I wanted my life to be. I had no idea how I would get there and often times doubted that I ever would. I can directly pinpoint when my life began to change. It was when I intensified my prayer life. I prayed more often and more fervently. I examined the scriptures more closely and made requests based on what was already promised. I mostly prayed for lost souls, broken relationships, and for the Lord to transform my life and use it for His glory. After I decided that I was willing to allow the Lord to use me fully, I became bold with my requests for other things, such as having a business and what kind of house I wanted. I felt confident in asking Him for exactly what I wanted because I was fully submitted to Him and His will for my life.

I prayed these prayers thinking that it would be a while before they were answered, but things started happening immediately in my marriage, in the lives of my children, and my extended family members. Then He began to answer my prayers about things that I dreamed of, such as being a business owner. Things started moving overwhelmingly fast. It was exciting, but I was thinking, "Slow down, Lord." What He gave me to know was that all the things that I had prayed for in the past and recently, were now being released. Why? I was seeking Him diligently, relentlessly, and expecting (which is faith) based on His word. He spoke to my spirit: "Didn't you know that I would do it?" In the past, I was not preparing for what I was praying for. So now I was scrambling, trying to keep up with how quickly the Lord was moving in my life.

I began to prepare for what I prayed for. My husband was working midnights, so I was able to accomplish a lot in the late hours of the night. I read books, researched and developed ideas. I was more focused than I had ever been in my life. The Lord began to send people to me. He was speaking to me more than ever before.

I began to set my alarm to wake up earlier. I made sure that I was dressed and prayed up before my children got up. When I was prepared, He would have something new for me. More opportunities came my way because my life was in order, and I was expecting something from Him. Follow these steps and you are guaranteed to live in your purpose and experience true fulfillment.

Chapter 9

Caring For Yourself

There role of wives and mothers are extraordinary. When you understand all that God has put within us, you will understand why the enemy wants us to believe that we are missing out on something or being held back. Eve fell for it. We know better. In addition to serving and warring in the spirit, the Lord wants us to care for ourselves. Our bodies need to be healthy and fit for our calling. We must continue to cultivate our gifts and talents. We need to develop and maintain healthy relationships with other women who can challenge and encourage us. I must interject that encouragement is not just for when you're weary and sad. Some of us need to take courage and live in our purpose as opposed to mediocrity. Most importantly, for self-care we must stay at the feet of Jesus. We need to read the word and pray so that we stay in the spirit.

There is only one way possible to manage your household in both the spiritual and natural realms: through the power of the Holy Spirit. Without His wisdom you won't even see what needs to be done. Without His power, you won't stand a chance at trying to accomplish the will of

The Father. It is imperative to make time to spend with Him.

Many Christian women struggle on a daily basis with guilt and shame because they aren't giving God His time. There's a false image going around about what time with God looks like. You have to get up at 6 a.m., study and take notes, then pray for a least an hour, right? Well, this is only one picture out of the full reality. At some stages of your life, time with the Lord may look like that. Those who are stuck with that one image will likely struggle when life changes. When you have children or anything else in your life that makes it impossible for you to have a static routine, time with the Lord gets really creative.

When I had one child, I had my quiet time with the Lord at her nap time every day. It was great. That changed when I had the second baby. With a toddler and a newborn, I was sleepless. It was like they were tag teaming me. When I finally got the baby to sleep, the toddler would wake up for lunch. I spent years feeling guilty and lukewarm. The truth was, I was not giving God His time, but it was because I felt like it had to be that perfect image or nothing at all.

The enemy was condemning me and holding me captive: "Why pray now? You've already started the day. How are you going to pray to God while you're cleaning up. Oh now you want to pray before bed. So you're giving God the last of yourself." These are the things that the enemy says to condemn and discourage me.

The Lord does give us grace in rough seasons, but that grace does not come in the form of a pass out of prayer and reading of the word. Prayer and reading is not a homework assignment from God. It is a gift from God to help us. We learn about who He is and how to navigate the world. How much you read and pray is the extent to which you will experience more of Him: His freedom, power, wisdom, joy, love, and peace. We have no defense against the enemy when our spirit man is starving. You can't call time out on the kingdom of darkness. They don't play fair. In fact, they come for you the hardest when you are in seasons of transition or difficulty.

Sometimes God, in His graciousness, will choose the meeting time and call us into prayer when He knows it's the best time. The purpose may be for our own good or because we need to intercede on behalf of someone else. The Lord is always speaking, but when our spirit man is weakened, it is difficult to hear Him. These are the times that the Lord will get our attention in other ways. Maybe your children will wake up and come to your room saying something unintelligible. You may find yourself repeatedly waking up at the same time in the middle of the night and unable to go back to sleep. Your husband may leave for work very early and you are unable to get back to sleep. You may abruptly awaken for no apparent reason. These are some of the ways in which The Lord may be trying to call you into prayer so that he can talk to you.

When our prayer life is strong, we hear from the Lord clearly and quickly because there is an established line of communication. Sometimes we think that God is silent, when the problem is that we can't hear Him. A weak prayer life is like leaving home without a cell phone. Someone may need help or they could be trying to tell you that you are headed for trouble. Since they can't contact you directly, they have find other ways to communicate.

A few months ago, my husband's cell phone screen had gone black. It was a touch screen phone so he couldn't use it much. If the phone rang, he could not answer it, but he could make calls through voice commands. When I needed to contact him, I had to get creative. I would call him three times in a row so he would know it was me. Then he would know to call me back. Sometimes I would have to call the person who I knew he would be with and ask them to have him call me. When he called back, I may have asked him to get something for me or tell him that he forgot something. Communication is imperative. Prayer is communication.

Offer God the best of what you have. When God asked for the first fruits, he didn't say unless you have a bad season. If out of a full harvest, there were only ten good ears of corn, he didn't demand twelve; He just wanted the best of the ten. During the writing of this book was the absolute most difficult season of my life. Honestly, it was a season where I had to decide whether I even wanted to serve the Lord anymore. I also heard from God like never before. It was the most fruitful season of my entire life. This book is one of the ripest picks. Well, all that God birthed in me was not conceived in a window seat with coffee, a blanket, and my bible.

My most powerful encounters with the Lord were in the laundry room. I don't know how it began, but I found myself crying out to God every time I went to put a load in. My kids would be at the vent upstairs, listening. I also had some breakthroughs while driving and some while showering. At that time, I prayed more frequently and more boldly than ever, and it was for different lengths of time, in different places, and with different intensities.

All God needs is your undivided attention, and if you are hungry enough for His presence, nothing can distract you. Remember, the Lord made women with a remarkable ability to multitask. If we can hold a phone to our ears while dressing a child, then we can pray while making breakfast. We put people on speaker phone so that we can work while we talk. Put the word on audio so you can listen to the word while folding laundry. That is God's grace for seasons of busyness and irregularities. You will have that ideal time with the Lord in another season.

The demands of a family are endless. After God, our families should get the best of our time. However, they should not get all of our time. We need time outside of the home so that we can regroup and even have the chance to miss them. Sometimes when the pressure mounts, you can feel like you are ready to implode, and just a two hour outing can reset you. Just go anywhere alone so that you can rest your mind.

It's important to have healthy relationships with women who share your lifestyle. Married or single, children or not, every woman needs to have a relationship with another woman who understands. You don't need to be around anyone who will assist you in tearing down your own house. When you hang around people who build you up, you will go home with a desire to love your family more.

Saying No

Often times, women do not know how to say no. We feel guilty that we didn't try harder to make a way out of no way. We tend to think that it's only okay to say no if it's impossible for us to do something. I have learned to say no in many ways and why it's important.

When we say yes all the time, we train people to think that we are superwoman. When we are always operating at maximum capacity, everyone thinks that we can handle it, so they add on more. People tend to ask for help from the person who says yes the most. It's not always the case that we are being abused or taken advantage of. Sometimes it's our own fault that people ask so much of us and give so little back.

We want our families to have the best, but there must be a balance between what God requires and what they can recognize. If you give what people do not have the capacity to appreciate, then you will be left feeling unappreciated (this concept also goes back to the marriage chapter: serving in the right areas). Similarly, we need to be careful about how much we give our children. If they are not able to appreciate what you give them or do for them, then you should not give it. You will hurt yourself and impede their growth.

Mothers very often put themselves last for the sake of their children. That is normal, but there must be balance. A mother is called to serve her children, but not as a peasant. We have needs and wants, too. You should reserve some things for you only. Then, your children will understand that they are not entitled to everything that you have. It starts with little things like food. My children beg for every crumb that they see. Some things I do not share with them. It's not about food, but about teaching them that mama likes to enjoy things, too. If I do share anything from my personal stash with them, they will appreciate it because it's a rare occurrence.

At lunch time, I would usually let the children eat the leftovers from dinner. If there wasn't much left, I would just find something else to eat. Well, after so many times of going without, my oldest just factored me out completely. She would distribute the food amongst herself and her siblings and totally disregard me. She would say "It was only enough for us" or "I didn't know you wanted any." Her way of thinking was my fault. By giving them the last of everything, I taught them that I didn't really need food. My daughter even told me "I didn't think you cared about food." What human being doesn't care about food?

To change this flawed thinking, sometimes I would take the most desired food and give them the lesser. By lesser I mean a fish taco versus peanut butter and jelly. Sometimes I will just divide everything up among us all. Everyone may only have a little bit, but as children who eat five to six times a day, no one will die. Besides, I think it's good for kids who live in abundance to experience hunger pangs every once in a while. It's a good reminder of how blessed they are.

If I want to leave the house alone and they ask to go with me, I say no and I make the reason clear: "I am with you all the time, I want to be alone." Sometimes I get overstimulated with noise and touching. Instead of enduring the torture until bedtime, I just say, "Look, I'm overstimulated and I don't want to talk to anyone or look at anything right now." I want them to understand that I am mama but I, too, have feelings. I also want to teach them to respond to body language that says "I don't want to be bothered." We should have self-control, but we should not hide our emotions so much so that they do not consider our feelings. That will only make them think that we can handle more than what we actually can.

When my kids would ask me what I wanted as a gift for Mother's Day or Christmas, like many moms I would say, "Oh, baby, you don't have to get me anything. It's the thought that counts." Well, I learned that was only teaching them that I didn't care about gifts. I started answering their offers with real desires that required money. Mama doesn't want another gift from her own closet. Earn money and buy me something. Clearly, I don't need them to support me. Kardell buys me whatever I want. I want them to know that I like things, too. The greater lesson to be learned is that a gift should reflect not just a thought, but effort as well. I like a good homemade gift, but I will only keep the things that show effort.

We have to say no to things outside of the home that drain us. We have other family members, friends, school, work, and church that all compete for our time. If outside service is in the way of family service, then we must say no. If that means, postponing your degree, quitting your job, telling grandma or the church no, then so be it. Take care of home first.

Your family wants to see you happy and refreshed. God wants you to enjoy his creation. It is important to let your children see you in another light. If your children only see you as a servant, then how will that shape their definition of a woman? A wife? A mother? Will your son expect his wife to only serve? Will your daughter dread marriage and motherhood? Does your husband see you as a bitter and burned out maid, or his wife who gracefully plays many roles? Love God first so that you can love yourself in Him. The only way to successfully manage a household in the realm of the natural, as well as the spirit, is by the love, power, and wisdom of God. Seek Him first.

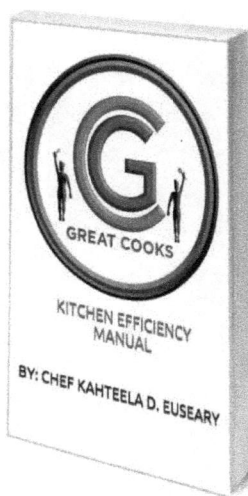

GREAT COOKS

KITCHEN EFFICIENCY MANUAL

BY: CHEF KAHTEELA D. EUSEARY

ISBN-10: 0692807195

ISBN-13: 978-0692807194

There are a lot of skills involved in managing a kitchen. Unfortunately, previous generations failed to pass down these skills. As a result many people dread cooking, can't find the time or just can't seem to make things run smoothly. Great Cooks Kitchen Efficiency Manual is a quick learning tool to teach home cooks how to consistently produce nourishing meals with limited waste of time, effort or resources.. This books offers tips on budgeting, saving money, shopping, menu planning, education on what foods are healthy to eat, kitchen equipment and kitchen organization. You are one read away from well- run kitchen.

For more wisdom and encouragement, visit the The Godly Household Manager Blog and subscribe to the newsletter!

Thegodlyhm.com

Email: info@thegodlyhm.com

www.ingramcontent.com/pod-product-compliance
Lightning Source LLC
LaVergne TN
LVHW091219080426
835509LV00009B/1067